W9-BXE-541

WITHDRAWN

Louder and Funnier

WITHDRAWN

LOUDER AND FUNNIER

A Practical Guide For Overcoming Stagefright In Speechmaking

ROBERT B. NELSON

1🐝

TEN SPEED PRESS
Berkeley, California

PN
4121
.N427
1985

1�)
TEN SPEED PRESS
P O Box 7123
Berkeley, California 94707

Library of Congress Catalog Number: 85-2575
ISBN: 0-89815-142-2

Book Design by Nancy Austin
Cover Design by Brenton Beck

Printed in the United States of America
10 9 8 7 6 5 4 3 2 1

Acknowledgements

Thanks to Brad Thompson and Anne Carroll for their work on the Pragmatic Publications edition of this book; David Dotlich for his invaluable insights and suggestions for revisions; Paul Scheele who helped me to overcome my stagefright and provided the impetus for many of the topics dicussed within; Walter Mink for suggesting the title; Jackie Wan for organizational improvements and editing to the Ten Speed Press edition; and Nancy Austin for assisting with the artwork.

Contents

Introduction

It's not difficult to recall the feeling—your heart is pounding, your breath is too short to catch, your mouth is full of cotton, your hands are so wet the papers you're clutching are curling, the voices around you are a numbing roar. . . and suddenly that stranger miles away at the front of the room announces your name.

It's all over.

You melt in the flame of faces staring at you, ooze out of your chair and slither up to the podium. If you are lucky, sounds come out of your mouth.

You vow to never again accept a speaking engagement.

Sound familiar?

Congratulations! You're normal.

The anxiety and apprehension you feel is like that thousands of other speakers experience under similar circumstances. You can overcome the fear you have of speaking before others and you can do it with this book you are holding. *Louder and Funnier* is a straightforward guide to speaking without fear. It is simply organized in three sections. The first section, "Preparing for the Stage," helps you to understand and analyze your speaking fears and to develop a plan for overcoming stagefright. The second section, "In the Limelight," focuses on controlling and channeling your anxiety while you are speaking. The last section, "After the Applause," examines additional skills and theories to consider for long-term resolutions to your fear of speaking. The appendix provides a capsule guide to preparing and organizing presentations; it can be used long after your fear of speaking has vanished.

Speaking to a group is one of the rare opportunities we have to impress many people within a relatively short period of time. If that group is made up of individuals who are important to us, such as our manager, others above us in the organization or even our peers, the desire to do well in our presentation is very great. After all, if we do a professional job and demonstrate an ability to think quickly on our feet, it is bound to be an asset when organizational rewards are allocated. This is painfully obvious to us when we realize that a presentation is one of the few times that we have any contact at all with many of those individuals above us in an organization.

The upcoming material will give you insight into understanding and overcoming stagefright so you can feel more comfortable speaking before groups and communicate more effectively. A systematic model for handling your fear will be explained as will the most effective known "cures" for stagefright. Emphasis will be placed on controlling stagefright symptoms, and dozens of techniques will be presented for you to explore. Methods for permanently overcoming the problem will also be discussed. While almost everyone responds to speaking situations with some anxiety, one of the key differences between a good public speaker and an inexperienced public speaker is the ability to control and manage stagefright. Fear is harnessed by the effective speaker in the process to be discussed in this book.

To simplify our discussion, several terms will be used to refer to the situation of speaking to a group throughout this book. A "presentation" will refer to a formal, prepared speech, usually in business or for a group such as a staff meeting or conference, scheduled in advance with prior knowledge of the topic. A "speech" will also be considered formal, usually to a group of 10 to 20 individuals, but with a wider range of purposes such as an entertaining or educational meeting. A "talk" will refer to speaking to a group of people on an informal basis and at times without advance notice. The use of the term "speaking" will always refer to speaking to a group unless otherwise stated, such as one-to-one speaking or speaking on the telephone.

I. Preparing for the Stage

Understanding Stagefright

John is a sociable, outgoing person. He makes friends easily and enjoys talking informally with people about his family, job and current events. He actually spends most of the day speaking in one way or another on the telephone, in meetings, with his family and even to strangers on the bus while coming to work. He would lead a comfortable life, except he has one major fear: speaking to groups.

John turns pale at the thought of talking to a group, and his good nature quickly vanishes. It is replaced with a fear that seems to possess him, taking control of his mind and seemingly his body. He doesn't act or even feel like himself as long as the possiblity of a public presentation is looming near. . . or far. He takes great efforts to avoid the impending doom. He first tries to politely decline the task of speaking before others, then he creates excuses and, if necessary, even fakes an illness to avoid making a public presentation. His fear does not seem logical, but he knows that it is very real for him and it causes him great discomfort.

Julie has a similar reaction to speaking to groups. She fears the activity so much that she has intentionally made career decisions to minimize her chances of being called upon to speak in front of others. She once wanted to go into management, but she knew that would mean giving talks to groups above and below her in the organization. She recently declined another promotion.

Julie also plans her social life around stagefright. She refuses to be an officer of any club and avoids large parties where she will likely have to talk informally to a group of people. She finds herself so afraid of the prospect of having to talk to a group that she avoids thinking about or preparing for the task when a speaking situation is inevitable. Her lack of preparation shows: she appears to be ill-prepared and/or unknowledgeable about the topic to members of the audience. Her confidence falls with each presentation she gives.

After each performance, her determination to avoid future public speaking situations is renewed. Her sole focus when confronted with a new speaking opportunity becomes a desperate attempt to avoid the task. The weeks and even months preceding a presentation become totally disrupted; she loses sleep, seems unable to relax and becomes generally miserable and unproductive in all aspects of her life.

John and Julie are like millions of other Americans who are affected by stagefright every day. You are the exceptional case if you do not experience some degree of stagefright, nervousness, or anxiety prior to, during or after a presentation. In fact, speaking to groups has consistently appeared as the number one fear of Americans in nationwide surveys over the past several years. Seventy percent consider themselves shy, and are unlikely to assert themselves in speaking situations.

Why is it we are perfectly comfortable talking to individuals or even to a total stranger while alone with him, yet as soon as one or more persons enter the conversation, we begin to have problems with the simple process of speaking? We surely did not forget such a natural skill which, like other skills such as walking or eating, has become second nature to us. Like those skills, we typically pay no attention at all to the process of speaking while we are doing it. . . until others are watching us. We spend hours talking in one form or another almost every day, yet when in front of a group it often seems we can't speak normally. When we stand up, our brain sits down.

What can be done to understand, cope with, and overcome stagefright? Answers to these questions and many others lie on the pages ahead. . .

What Is Stagefright?

Stagefright is the nervousness we experience before an audience. In a mild form, it can be a slight uneasiness or "butterflies in our stomach." In a more serious form, it can be a devastating phobia. Individuals report a wide range of stagefright anxieties. Some are nervous for months before a presentation, some get nervous during a presentation, and a few even experience a wave of anxiety after they are done speaking.

We feel that we are taking a risk when we speak before others. Even if we know the audience members well (and sometimes *because* we know them well) the situation is stressful. We are exposing our thoughts and beliefs in a short amount of time to a number of different individuals. Our ideas, logic, and even our values are placed on display. We feel that we are risking our reputation with those we respect, and the consequences can seem enormous. If we fail we will face many of the same individuals the next day. Just as a successful presentation can have a positive impact on our career, a poor presentation can seem to have a negative impact. When it's OUR poor presentation, the negative impact seems as if it is terminal.

We fear we have to live up to the expectations of others. And perhaps toughest of all—our own expectations. Most speakers want to do a good job. In fact, you are more likely to have stagefright if you want to do a good job. A slip of the tongue, a poor word selection or·mispronounced word may seem to be a major flaw to people who are being hypercritical of themselves, although it is likely not to even be noticed by members of the audience.

This increased self-consciousness amplifies every part of the speaking process. Since we are concerned about doing our best, we look for and see the worst in ourselves. Every flaw, hesitancy or nervous symptom becomes a serious mistake in our mind's eye, capable of undermining our confidence.

When the consequences of failure seem great, our imagination becomes more vivid about the ways we are apt to make mistakes. We become so preoccupied with failure, it soon becomes inevitable. We become caught up in a self-fulfilling prophecy.

Instead of encouraging ourselves, we tend to criticize ourselves when we are in a less confident situation. As we speak to a group we critically analyze our speech. We mentally tell ourselves that we are making mistakes as we go along: "What a stupid remark."—"They look confused. I must be going too fast."—"Jones is still mad about that project from two months ago; I'll collapse if he tries to nail me on this next point."—"One person yawned and another looked at her watch—I must really be bombing."

Such hypercriticism in a suggestive frame of mind is apt to cause even the best speaker to question his or her ability to effectively communicate. These critical observations must be turned into positive motivations or totally ignored if you want to succeed in a given speaking situation. Your attention must be focused on communicating your material—what you have to say—not on finding fault with your delivery when you first open your mouth. You must focus on making speaking to groups a natural, conversational process, not an intimidating, infrequent occurrence that is to be feared and avoided at all costs.

What we fear in a speaking situation will vary from individual to individual. A common reason given by many speakers, as I said earlier, is a fear of not doing as well as we would like to do. This can be due to feeling that we don't know what we are doing, remembering that we did not do well the last time we spoke, believing that others expect us to do better than we are able to do, or feeling that we may not have control of ourselves or the situation.

We fear rejection and evaluation by other people, especially those individuals who have power over us, such as a manager at our place of employment. We fear not doing well in front of those who are important to us. We fear the potential for rejection, whether it is expressed or not. We fear what people will think, feel and say about us, even if those people are complete strangers. We fear having a lowered self-esteem. We fear being the center of attention because of the possibility of being embarrassed in front of others.

We fear the future consequences of doing a less than satisfactory job. At work, it might make our job more difficult if it is discovered that we are ineffective in speaking situations. We may lose the favorable opinion of those who have an influence on our success in the company. In social situations, it may affect the number of friends we have and how much we enjoy social settings. It might even affect how much others enjoy having us around.

Misconceptions about Stagefright

To better understand stagefright we should first clarify some common misconceptions about the topic. Here are three key facts about stagefright:

FACT #1: **Stagefright is a normal, healthy feeling.** Not only do most people experience stagefright, but it would be abnormal for you not to. It is your body's way of alerting you to be prepared. The more important the speaking situation is to you, the more nervous you are likely to be. Without anxiety, you would have little energy or enthusiasm about the speaking situation, and would likely come across as a very boring speaker to your audience. Some speakers who do not become anxious also run the risk of being inappropriate in the speaking situation, that is, offending the audience, using humor in bad taste, or rambling. Their lack of concern for doing a good job makes them oblivious to the audience's reaction. Such an outlook on public speaking is far more detrimental than stagefright and much more difficult to correct. Be glad you are anxious in speaking situations!

FACT #2: Stagefright seems more severe to the speaker than the audience. Symptoms of stagefright are amplified by the speaker who is looking for them. A small speaking error seems like a major mistake when we are nervous. For example, a speaker may become aware that his or her hands are shaking and will think it is noticeable to the audience. This will make the person more uneasy, causing his or her hands to shake even more, as well as other symptoms of stress to appear. This cycle has the potential of escalating to the point where the speaker becomes so distracted by nervous symptoms that they become a barrier to communication with the audience and he or she cannot continue. Actually, few symptoms can be detected by the audience members, and those symptoms that can be seen rarely detract from the presentation.

FACT #3: Stagefright tends to escalate the more we seek to escape it. One of the ironies about stagefright is that the more we try to avoid it, the more we are likely to experience it. We fear when we most want not to fear. Instead of trying to hide from fear in a speaking situation, we need to become comfortable with being uncomfortable. We need to accept the feeling of fear as being legitimate and be confident that it will quickly pass rather than let it distract us from our purpose. We need to continue ignoring negative symptoms and, instead, seek positive reinforcement, such as giving ourselves a "pep talk" prior to speaking or complimenting ourselves during or after a presentation. We must come to a truce with fear rather than fight a battle we cannot win.

The Nature of Fear

Most fears are thought to be rooted in the "fight or flight" syndrome of prehistoric man. When he was faced with a threat, his response was either to flee from the danger or to stay and fight it. For example, if he came across a wild animal, he had to make a decision to fight it (perhaps he had no choice in the matter) or run from it. In either case, extra energy was needed fast, so his body pumped extra adrenalin into his bloodstream.

We have entered an age in which most of our fears are imagined and fewer of them are real. Speaking is just one such imagined fear. There is no physical harm that befalls even a bad speaker, only the imagined threats of what others might think or the potential consequences of failure. When faced with these perceived dangers, we receive the same rush of energy, but we do not need to use it. Instead, we stand and feel it build within us to the point where it inhibits our ability to perform. This extra energy makes us "jumpy" and distorts our sense of perception—at its worst, it can be debilitating.

Many people come to fear the feeling of nervousness and let that fear be a constant part of their life—even when no speaking situation is close at hand. They "fear the fear" of being afraid.

Fear is an emotion that is often irrational and seems to be out of our control when we are in its grips. The feeling of helplessness is precisely why and what we come to fear. To cope with fear, you need to understand what you fear and plan a strategy to overcome your fear. Trying to deal with fear without a plan is not likely to be successful. Like a Chinese finger trap, the harder you try to escape, the more it grips you.

Levels of Fear

You may never have stopped to think that fear can have different levels of intensity. We usually think in terms of being either anxious or not being anxious, almost as if a switch were thrown inside us. But there is a difference between being scared and being scared to death.

Fear has different levels of intensity. If you learn to be sensitive to the different levels of fear, you will be better able to catch yourself at earlier stages and keep your fear from escalating. For our purposes here, let's define three levels of fear from the greatest intensity to the least intensity.

LEVEL I: Hysterical. The most severe level of fear is an irrational, excessive, and persistent fear of speaking. A person who fears speaking that much tries to avoid, at all costs, that which is feared by making excuses, planning time conflicts and possibly even becoming physically ill. The symptoms are hysteria, total unwillingness to deal with the situation, and, at times, paranoia. When unreasoning fear strikes quickly, the resulting feeling is panic. If I had a Level I fear of crime, for example, I might have 20 padlocks on my front door, iron bars on all the windows, two burglar alarm systems, and an armed guard, and I would avoid leaving home.

LEVEL II: Scared. When we consciously seek to avoid what we fear and have physical symptoms that detract from our abilities, we have a level of fear that is irrational, yet could be overcome. The symptoms include blurred vision, pale complexion, and nausea. When we are scared, we often "freeze" or run away from the situation. When I am scared of being mugged, I walk faster and may hear my heart pounding in my ears.

LEVEL III: Nervous. When we spend time worrying about what we fear but have a natural reaction that subsides, we are nervous about speaking. The symptoms are less noticeable and distracting and may include a dry mouth, sweaty palms and/or a faster rate of talking. I am nervous about crime when I regularly watch the paper for information which supports my belief.

Benefits of Fear

Few people ever stop to consider what the advantages of fear are. Instead, fear is most often dreaded because it seems only to deter from our effectiveness in speaking situations. When we have a great deal of fear, we usually do a poor job of speaking. Most of our instincts, however, have value, and fear is no exception. Take a moment and consider what would happen if you were not fearful when speaking to groups.

If you had absolutely no fear or anxiety about speaking to a group, you would probably be completely calm. The audience may then perceive you as having a "who cares" attitude, or may even consider you cocky and arrogant. An audience usually assumes the mood and energy level of the speaker. Since we usually do, in fact, care about what happens, it is good to show a certain amount of concern. This concern is often seen by the audience as energy—an excitement and enthusiasm on the part of the speaker.

What would happen during your delivery if your attitude and behavior did not indicate that you were "concerned?" You might come across as being too casual or flippant. Many speakers who have no fear come across in a very reckless fashion. They make inappropriate remarks or jokes and use poor examples; they complain or criticize the audience; they ramble and generally abuse their audience's time; they often appear to be unprepared or boring; they show little respect for the situation. This attitude might be insulting to members of your audience who are expecting you to show them or the topic more respect. If they walk away from the meeting thinking that you were a smart aleck, you will not have left a favorable impression.

Fearing and worrying, then, do have advantages that serve to protect you. Worrying is a reminder that you have preparation to do; it gives you extra energy for that preparation. Thus, the more we want to do our best, the greater our fear is apt to be. You should be glad that this is the case. I hope that you always will retain enough anxiety about a speaking situation to want and try to do your best.

Speaking before others is in almost all cases a significant event for each of us. Whether we are trying to sell an idea, impress someone in the audience, or entertain a group of friends, the situation is likely to be important to us. To the extent that we are concerned about others, and concerned with making a quality presentation, speaking will be important—and a bit scary—to us. To have it differently would perhaps be scariest of all.

Analyzing Your Fears

Although you probably don't think so now, your fear of speaking is not a permanent problem. There are techniques to learn and skills to develop that will help you overcome your stagefright. In order to deal with your problem most effectively, though, the first thing you need to do is pinpoint the source of your fears. This section presents a variety of approaches for analyzing your fears.

Looking Back

If you are afraid to speak to a group now, it is probably safe to assume you were afraid the last time you spoke to a group. But can you remember the time before that? Can you remember the very first time that you were fearful about speaking to a group? Can you remember the instant you first felt the fear? Can you reexperience that exact instant?

I think you can. Close your eyes and picture where you were. Try to use all of your senses in recreating your experience. Were you sitting or standing? Can you feel your physical environment? Who was in the room? Can you see their faces? Can you see their expressions? What noises could you hear? What were you talking about? Were others talking? Was there a crystal-clear silence?

Now, slowly relive the experience. What was the first clue you had that something was not right? Was it a change of a facial expression in the crowd? Or noticing something unpleasant was happening to your body, such as tensing in your muscles? What happened next? What was your reaction to the realization that something was different? Did you give a nervous laugh or mentally say something to yourself? If so, did your action or thought make continuing any easier? If it did not, stop and imagine what else you could have done that would have made continuing easier. Perhaps asking if there were any questions or asking a question of the audience would have helped. Perhaps giving a summary of what you had said so far, or stopping to look at your notes to see what you should say next. Perhaps mentally telling yourself that this new, uncomfortable feeling is odd, but certainly nothing to worry about. Perhaps calling for a break or concluding your presentation. Try one of these alternatives now as you relive your first speaking fear.

You need to realize that your fear is not an automatic reflex, but an habitual, learned response that you have chosen to go along with each time you speak. This habit developed much the same way any bad habit does, through repetition and reinforcement. But habits can be broken. You can learn to substitute more desirable behavior when the same circumstances occur again. You can chose to react differently.

Fearful Situation Assessment

Knowing where you are now will help you plan a strategy for overcoming your fears. This inventory lists different types of speaking situations, from the most comfortable to the most frightening. Where do you fall on the scale? How far would you like to go? Chances are you will find grey areas where it is difficult to tell exactly how many more people will make a situation scary, for example, but this inventory will still give you an idea as to where you stand right now, and where to begin your road to improved speaking. Starting from where you are comfortable, you must focus your energy on moving up to the next level of difficulty.

CHECK ✔ those speaking situations you most fear:

_____ Talking to yourself

_____ Talking to your plants

_____ Talking to your cat or dog

_____ Talking to a family member

_____ Talking to a friend

_____ Talking on the telephone

_____ Talking to a stranger

_____ Talking to two family members

_____ Talking to two friends

_____ Talking to three friends or family members

_____ Talking to two strangers while sitting

_____ Talking to your manager

_____ Talking to two strangers while standing

_____ Talking to more than three friends while sitting

_____ Talking into a microphone

_____ Talking at a staff meeting where you work

_____ Presenting negative information to anyone

_____ Giving a planned presentation to two people at work

_____ Talking to a group of friends at a social gathering, standing

_____ Talking to three to five strangers by chance

_____ Introducing yourself at a training session to a group of 20 people

_____ Being video taped

_____ Giving a presentation to three to five strangers

_____ Giving a presentation at your staff meeting

_____ Talking to a reporter

_____ Giving a presentation at your staff meeting with your manager present

_____ Giving a presentation at someone else's staff meeting above you in the organization

_____ Talking on a radio program

_____ Giving a prepared speech to a civic organization

_____ Speaking on a TV program

_____ Giving a prepared speech to a professional organization

_____ Being asked to give a presentation for a conference

_____ Being told to give a presentation at a conference

_____ Other:

Your Speaking Beliefs

Most of our behavior can be traced to underlying beliefs we hold about our reality. When you periodically examine and contrast those beliefs, you might find that some of them are conflicting. Fear, and its symptoms, doubt and procrastination, are some of the behavioral outlets of conflicting beliefs which you hold to be mutually important. When you understand what your beliefs are, speaking fears are less apt to be mysterious.

We already know that you believe speaking to groups is frightening, and the degree to which you are frightened will show in your symptoms. Buy why are you frightened? Why do you not enjoy speaking to groups? Chances are it is because you believe one or more of the following statements is true.

- I don't think I'm very good at it.

- I might not do well. Others will think less of me.

- My fear inhibits and paralyzes me.

- I'm shy.

- I hate being observed.

- I am too awkward and will probably embarrass myself.

- I don't know what to do. I don't know how to prepare or what to say.

Now ask yourself why you want to be unafraid, why you want to enjoy speaking to groups. Your answer might sound like:

- I need to be able to get my ideas across clearly and effectively.

- I have to do a good job in front of others, especially if those others are important to me.

- My job requires that I make occasional presentations.

- I know that speaking to groups is an essential skill in positions of high responsibility, and I hope to advance to those levels.

Now, where might these two sets of beliefs be in conflict? An obvious conflict would be if it is important for you to speak to others in your job, but you do not think you can do it. In order for you to be able to give presentations in your job without fear, you will have to change one of these two beliefs: either you will have to believe it is not important for you to be able to speak to groups in your job, or you'll have to believe that you are fully capable of speaking to groups in your job. Once you restructure the fabric of your beliefs, your behavior and actions will quickly follow.

In the first case, if you decide that speaking in your job is not important to you, you will be less concerned about how you are perceived in a speaking situation, and won't care if you are not perceived as a great speaker. If you care less, you will be less anxious. Although this is a good rationalization to gain perspective (that is, the world won't end if you fail), it is not always a viable option. For example, your manager may believe, or expect you to believe, that speaking is an important part of your job. Then you would have to either change your manager's belief, or find another manager who agrees with your priorities.

How much more positive it would be to start believing that you *can* speak to groups and do a fine job of it. Your first reaction to such a statement might be that it is absurd because you know for a fact that you are too scared to speak well. But imagine for a moment that you can speak without fear. What would be different in your behavior? Visualize yourself actually speaking to a group. What are you wearing? How are you standing? What do you see as you stand in front of them? Visualize them smiling and applauding—they really like you. If you develop a clear picture of what you want your behavior to be, it will be easier to bridge the gap between where you are now and where you want to be.

Let's examine your thoughts that lead to the final behavior. What would need to happen in order for you to believe—truly believe—that you can easily speak to a group without fear? Someone telling you that you do not need to be fearful might help. Telling yourself that your fear is unfounded might help even more. What would probably be of the greatest help, however, would be to actually experience a number of speaking situations in which your fear is absent: show yourself that it is possible to speak without fear and boost your confidence, and then do it enough additional times so that you can hardly remember—mentally or physically—what it was like to speak with fear.

The Fear Map

The "Fear Map" presented here offers a systematic means of overcoming stagefright. It enables you to pinpoint the variables that make you most fearful in speaking situations. Armed with a more precise awareness of what you do and do not fear, you will be able to overcome your weaknesses by using your strengths to comfortably move yourself into more difficult and fearful speaking situations.

Four broad areas are dealt with, each containing three specific factors. You can reach your desired state of comfort by "stretching yourself" in any of the areas that are troublesome for you. The process of improving should be less scary, since nothing is being forced upon you—the map is just a guide, and you can decide which direction to go and the speed at which you will progress. Multiple factors may be developed simultaneously, and suggestions will be made for ways to bridge the gap between your current and desired levels.

As you look at the map, imagine that you are at the center. You will be looking outward at the four areas which together make up the most relevant factors of your presentation: the

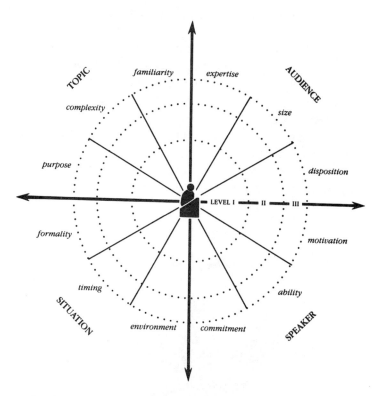

topic, the audience, the situation, and you, the speaker. Using the questions presented rank yourself on the specific variables within each area on a continuum from I to III:

Level I = high fear/low control of fear

Level II = moderate fear/moderate control of fear

Level III = low fear/high control of fear

The farther away you mark yourself from the center the greater control you have over that variable and the less fearful it is likely to be for you. The width of the bands corresponds to the relative difficulty of movement from the origin outward. It is typically more difficult to make an initial movement than it is to make subsequent movements, thus the band closer to the origin is wider.

Shade in the area from the center of the circle to your marked position for each of the 12 specific factors to obtain a graphic representation of your "sphere of control," the now-darkened area (see example below). The remaining white area will be your area of fear. Together they form your "fear map." The map will show where you currently are in contrast to where you want to be. The remaining white areas will represent the speaking variables you need to learn to control. The difference between where you are and where you want to be is your "confidence gap."

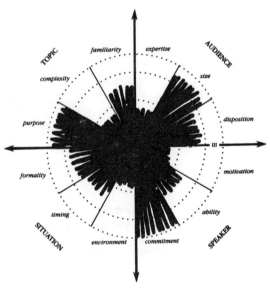

Sector One: The Topic

The first of the four general areas affecting a presentation is your comfort level with the topic. Your topic comfort level is usually a function of the difficulty of the topic, your familiarity with the topic, and the purpose of your presentation (i.e., what you hope to achieve).

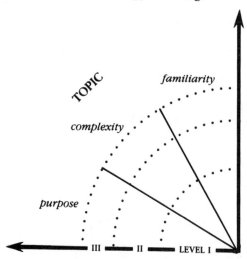

1. Complexity. At what level of complexity and/or abstraction are you comfortable speaking? Less complex topics include a description of a physical object or personal narrative (Level I). More complex topics include, for example, technical information, a discussion of government regulations, or economic theory (Level II). Abstract topics include, for example, presentations about freedom, the role of law in society, or social responsibility (Level III).

2. Familiarity. What level of familiarity with the topic do you need to be comfortable? Does it have to be very familiar, requiring little preparation, as is found in personal experiences or what you do for a living (Level I), or are you comfortable with speaking about topics that are relatively unknown to you (Level II)? Do you have to research and organize information or conduct extensive preparation (Level III)?

3. Purpose. How difficult is your purpose for speaking? Are you comfortable with describing events (Level I)? Can you explain a procedure or give detailed instructions (Level II)? Are you comfortable with giving a speech that entertains or persuades a group (Level III)?

Sector Two: The Audience

The second important variable affecting a presentation is your audience. How many people are in the audience? How much do they know about the topic? How strongly are they for or against the topic? These are all significant factors that influence the level of stress you will experience while speaking.

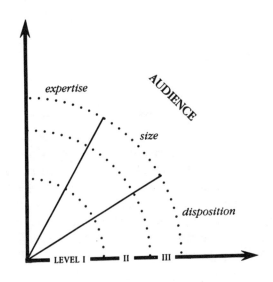

1. Group Size. With what size group do you become uncomfortable or fearful? Are you comfortable when speaking with a small group of less than five individuals (Level I) Can you easily talk to a group of 15–20 people (Level II)? Can you easily talk to large groups of 100 or more people (Level III)?

2. Expertise. At what level of expertise are you generally comfortable speaking? Does your level of comfort depend upon speaking about topics you know relatively more about than members of the audience (Level I)? Can you talk to groups who consist of people who know as much about the topic as yourself (Level II)? Can you address yourself to experts on the topic (Level III)?

3. Disposition. What is the likely disposition of the audience? How well do you know members of the audience? Do you have to know members of the audience well and have them like you to be at ease (Level I)? Are you comfortable speaking to acquaintances who voice contrary opinions and ideas (Level II)? Can you speak as easily to complete strangers whose disposition toward you and the topic is unknown or hostile (Level III)?

Sector Three: The Situation

In addition to the audience and topic, every presentation or speaking opportunity has a number of situational elements which affect the difficulty of the task. Your ability to control the amount of preparation time, the formality and the physical environment will affect your chances of success as well as influence your level of comfort.

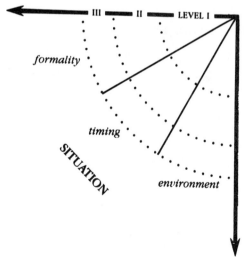

1. Time. The amount of time you have to prepare to speak can greatly affect the difficulty of a speaking situation. How much time do you have to prepare? Do you have a long period of time to prepare, say a week to a month (Level I)? Do you have two or three days to prepare (Level II)? Is the presentation extemporaneous or do you have less than a day's notice (Level III)?

2. Formality. Formal situations are considered by most speakers to be more difficult because there is less room for error. How formal is the speaking situation? Is the situation very informal, as in a toast among friends (Level I)? Are there time limits or a set agenda, as in a staff meeting (Leve II)? Is it a formal affair, as in hosting a banquet (Level III)?

3. Environment. Consider the extent to which you can manipulate and control the physical environment or unexpected circumstances. Can you easily handle losing your place in your notes or questions that can be anticipated (Level I)? Can you handle an unexpected event such as a projector that doesn't work or questions you can't answer (Level II)? Can you easily handle a major distraction, such as a heckler (Level III)?

Sector Four: The Speaker

The final variable of any speaking situation is the speaker—his or her speaking ability, motivation and level of commitment toward the task.

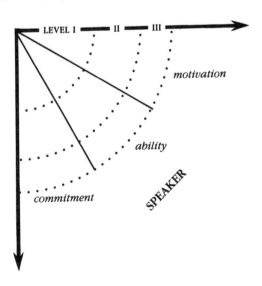

1. Experience. How experienced are you in speaking a) to groups, b) on this topic, and c) under these circumstances? If you are new to speaking before others all aspects may seem difficult (Level I). If it is new material, or a different audience, or an unfamiliar setting, speaking will be more difficult (Level II). If you have done the same presentation to a very similar group quite recently, this time will be easier (Level III).

2. Motivation. Motivation comes from within, and involves your ideals and goals. Part of it has to do with a desire to perform well—if it is important to you to do a great job, your motivation will always be high. Part of it may have to do with how enthusiastic or inspired you are by your topic—if you are speaking on a cause you consider vital, again, your motivation will be high. You don't really want to give this presentation at all? (Level I) You want to do a good job? (Level II) You want to excel, to make a strong impact? (Level III) (Note: For some individuals the order of difficulty may be reversed, that is it may be easier to speak before others when motivation is lacking entirely and very difficult when motivation is very high. In either case, if your level of motivation helps rather than hinders you, mark yourself farther from the center.)

3. Commitment. Your level of commitment is determined by your stated obligation to the task of speaking on this topic. This could range anywhere from your casually offering to say a few words at a small social gathering to your having signed a contract to make a lengthy speech before a large group. For example, would you be comfortable if *asked* to introduce members at a club meeting? (Level I) Would you be comfortable if your boss *assigns* you to give a sales presentation at the next meeting? (Level II) Would you be comfortable being a *paid* keynote speaker? (Level III) As with motivation (see above) the relationship between commitment and fear may be reversed for some people, but generally speaking, if you are highly committed you will have higher fear and lower comfort. Mark the map according to its effect on you.

Evaluating Your Strengths and Weakenesses

When you are finished with your map, you should have a graphic representation of your fear that is conveniently divided into areas that can be more easily addressed. The map will indicate your areas of greatest strength (the segments that are most blackened) and your weakest areas (the segments least blackened). You may find it helpful to list your top three or four fears, and your top three or four strengths as indicated by the Fear Map so that you can plan a strategy for improvement.

Greatest Strengths

1. _____

2. _____

3. _____

4. _____

Greatest Weaknesses

1. _____

2. _____

3. _____

4. _____

Developing a Plan for Overcoming Stagefright

A friend of mine once told me when asked how he overcame his fear of speaking to groups: "I was having lunch with a professor while visiting a college campus and he asked me if I would speak to his class after we finished eating. Assuming it was a small seminar, I agreed. I was surprised when I walked into a room of over 200 students, but managed to make it through an informal presentation. Since then, I have never had a problem."

One student I was assisting was very nervous when giving a casual talk about a topic of her choice to a small group. I asked her to describe the way she felt while standing in front of the group. She described the various symptoms of fear she felt. We surveyed the audience to see who noticed any of the symptoms that were described. None did. She was astonished to learn that fact, instantly relaxed and thereafter was able to be completely at ease.

These cases show that change can be easier than we first imagined, and is often just a matter of having additional information, additional experience, or approval for us to feel and behave differently. Perhaps it just takes a friend saying "Don't get nervous. Everything will be fine."

For most of us though these "quick solutions" do not work, and well-intentioned advice from those who have gotten over their fear may actually further alienate us. We might come to believe that perhaps our fear is not like the fear experienced by others. We may think our fear is abnormal. Don't be misled! Stagefright rarely disappears spontaneously just because someone tells us, "Everything's OK. Don't be afraid." For most of us, overcoming stagefright will take some hard work, planning, and a commitment to move forward.

What Do You Have Going for You?

I have never met a person who did not have some positive abilities and features to offer when speaking to a group. If you took the Fearful Situation Assessment (page 00) and filled in the Fear Map (pages 00 to 00) you already have some indications of your assets. Let's explore this aspect more thoroughly, though, as your strengths will serve as the foundation for developing confidence and a comfortable speaking style.

Past positive speaking experiences. To identify your past positive speaking experiences, review again your speaking history. This time, focus on what you did right. What was your most successful speaking experience? What is the largest group you ever spoke to before? What is the longest you ever spoke before a group, no matter if they were friends, family or strangers? When have you volunteered information in a classroom setting or lecture or simply asked a question? Give yourself credit for what you have achieved in speaking. Start to nurture your abilities and feel good about your strengths in front of a group. We have all done many things right in the past and will soon be doing even more to feel good about future speaking situations.

Current skills. Besides having a history of positive speaking experiences, albeit short, you also have a number of abilities and strengths related to speaking that you can build upon. Take inventory of them, because they can be used to your advantage. They might include:

Preparation Skills

- Well-organized
- Resourceful
- Timely
- Creative
- Persistent

Personality Features

- Interesting
- Likeable
- Exciting
- Gregarious
- Enthusiastic

Speaking Style

- Sincere
- Logical
- Candid
- Humble
- Insightful
- Humorous

Physical Features

- Neatly dressed
- Erect posture
- Good with gestures
- Steady smile
- Tall

Vocal Abilities

- Clear
- Loud
- Variable
- Pleasant

Others

_____

_____

_____

_____

_____

Your Plan for Speaking without Fear

Now that you have analyzed your ability to speak before groups and have some idea of where you would like to be, next you need only to plan a strategy for moving from your current state to your desired state.

Always work off your dimensions of strength, starting with those areas of greatest comfort and moving a step at a time closer to your goal. For example, if you are most fearful of speaking to a large group but very comfortable when speaking on a topic of great familiarity to you, plan to address increasingly larger groups about a topic you know better than the audience. This might mean volunteering to speak at a club meeting about an area of interest to you. Or the next time you need to make a presentation, make sure the topic is defined in such a way that you will be the authority.

If you are anxious about speaking to a group of three people or more, organize some information on a topic with which you are familiar, such as a hobby or current event, and present it to a few friends or family members. Then try it on a larger group of friends. Or, if you are planning a presentation to your staff, first deliver the presentation to a peer or your manager or your spouse. Determine the variables of your target speaking situation and try to simulate them as closely as possible.

At some point, you will be unable to simulate certain variables, such as a group of 200 people or questions from experts. Counteract your missing dimensions by intensifying other variables. For example, make up for not having 200 people by giving your presentation three times to different strangers. Simulate a group of experts. or top managers by giving a group of friends questions to ask you while you practice with them.

You must force yourself to accept risk and be willing to experiment with new behaviors. For instance, a person who has a strength in informally relating well with people could try to break down initial audience hostility by individually meeting people in the audience prior to the talk. Once he stands up in front of the group, he may recognize enough friendly faces to carry him through the presentation. (This technique has the added benefit of allowing the speaker to "test the waters" and find out what is on the audience's mind.) Some people will join a social or speaking group to build their number of speaking successes and level of experience. As they gain experience, they attempt more difficult topics, including practicing presentations that will be given at work.

As a matter of fact, one of the important aspects of your plan should be routine speaking every week. The nature and circumstances can vary, but the need to practice is essential. If you do not have an opportunity to speak to any groups at work one week, make an extra effort to speak in a social or civic activity you might attend. Or, have a conversation with a friend in a more structured, organized manner. Another option to consider is to join a club such as Toastmasters' International, which will give you an opportunity to speak frequently in a wide range of capacities. You need to develop your skills in speaking and controlling fear when you do not need to so that your skills are ready when you really need them. If your practice sessions are too infrequent, each occasion will seem as if you are starting over and your progress will be slower.

Use the following space to summarize what you have learned in this chapter.

1. Where I am now? (Describe the type of situation of greatest difficulty that you feel comfortable with):

2. Where I would like to be? (Describe the type of speaking situation that you would like to be able to handle well):

3. Which speaking strength(s) do I have that would help most?

4. What variable(s) are most fearful to me?

5. How can I use the strength(s) to overcome the weakness(es)?

Your plan to overcome your speaking fears will use the speaking strengths you have identified to diminish specific areas of speaking fears you have pinpointed. Each speaking success you have will then be used to further reduce speaking anxiety that you have. Your plan will repeatedly address specific fears so that you will be chipping away at your overall fear of speaking until your stagefright is gone.

II. In the Limelight

Getting Off to a Good Start

I recently had an individual tell me, "If I can just make it through the first two minutes of my presentation, I'll be fine." Most of us feel the same way. If we can somehow make it through our initial uneasiness without overreacting, losing the audience or totally blanking out, our preparation will come forth and rescue us. The longer we talk, the more our material sounds familiar to us and the greater our comfort level will be. If your beginning goes well, you are more apt to gain confidence and relax.

Of course, stagefright can creep up on us at any time during a presentation, not just at the beginning. You may be mentally congratulating yourself on having completed a fine presentation only to have an audience member rise to ask a question you are unprepared to answer causing you to panic. Suddenly you're back to Level I on the fear scale!

In this section you will find dozens of techniques to help you handle difficult moments at any stage of your presentation. There are tips to help you get through the crucial opening moments of your talk and through the question and answer period following a presentation. There are suggestions for ways to relax and build up confidence before your presentation and to control specific physical symptoms of stagefright while you are on stage. Preparation and practice should always be your primary tools in preventing stagefright, but it is still wise to have a few tricks up your sleeve as a backup. (See the appendix for general advice on speech preparation.)

Before You Start

Make plans to have the day of your presentation be a special day for you. Plan to feel good. Wear your favorite outfit that is appropriate for the occasion, buy yourself a present, and listen to some music that you enjoy prior to speaking. Give yourself rewards for progress in your preparation and plan a special event to celebrate the completion of your presentation. As much as possible, associate positive experiences and thoughts with the activity of speaking to groups.

As the time to speak draws near, psyche yourself into a positive, alert frame of mind. Imagine that from the moment you are in the room, or even the moment you get up that morning, that you are the center of attention. The controlled energy that you are intentionally placing in your body keeps you at your best, in contrast to uncontrolled nervous apprehension that accelerates as the presentation draws near. Tell yourself that you are ready even if there was more you could have done to prepare.

Neutralize excess energy. Individuals who are unsuccessful at controlling the nervous physical symptoms of stress should try to minimize their energy level. One way is to plan to be a little tired for your presentation. Your slight drowsiness will neutralize the excessive energy a fearful situation might bring on. The trade-off is that you are apt to seem less exciting and enthusiastic as a speaker. Excessive nervous energy prior to speaking can also be channelled into physical sport or activity. Besides being a nervous outlet, exercise can help to make you more resilient so that you can more easily bounce back from stressful situations.

Isometrics. If you have some privacy, you can perform some isometrics—exercises that involve muscle tension with little movement such as clasping your hands together and pushing as hard as possible. Many speakers always plan to step into a restroom immediately prior to speaking for isometrics, muscle tensing, and deep breathing exercises (page 53).

Meet the audience. If possible, prior to your presentation or meeting, try to establish physical contact with a good number, if not all, of the members of the group by shaking hands. If this is not possible, or if it would be awkward because you already know many of the individuals, mingle with as many members as possible before you start. This trick will help reduce any barriers you might be imagining and make the situation more natural.

Remember that you are the expert. You were asked to make this presentation or give this speech because someone recognized your expertise, either on this topic or before this group. Keep that in mind when you're feeling inadequate for the task. In addition, plan to reinforce this opinion of yourself by knowing your material thoroughly.

Think positive thoughts. If you are not prepared or suddenly realize that you have forgotten something, do not panic. It is too late to matter and chances are good that you will be able to proceed nicely without it. Do not make or consider changes in your opening lines either—it might throw you off.

Warm up your voice. Besides breathing exercises, muscle tension control, and isometrics you can do other physical activities to be sure you are ready when it is time to speak and have control of your environment while you are speaking. Many speakers make the mistake of not warming up their vocal muscles prior to a speaking situation. If you have ever talked to someone on the telephone after that person has just awakened, you know that it takes a few moments for your voice to warm up and be clearly audible. The same is true of speaking to a group. Do not wait until you are standing in front of 25 people to see if the volume of your voice is going to reach everyone.

Try your voice earlier that day in your car, in the shower, or in that same room before anyone arrives—try speaking very loudly without yelling. Your volume will be a direct result of the amount of air you are using to support your voice. Think of your voice as a ping-pong ball on top of a fountain of water. Your voice must be supported by a strong column of air.

Get your mouth muscles in tune. In a similar vein, wake up your ability to enunciate prior to the speaking situation, rather than fumbling with that ability in front of your audience. Try pronouncing the vowels of the alphabet very loudly and clearly several times or sing a song or two in the privacy of your home in the morning. Singing tends to emphasize vowel sounds more than speaking does, so that your speech will be clearer when you start your presentation. A final trick to play on your mouth muscles is drinking a citrus drink or swirling some lemon juice around in your mouth prior to your speaking engagement. This will snap your mouth muscles to attention and greatly improve your articulation.

Psyche yourself up. While waiting to speak, get enthusiastic about the situation. Think about why this group wants to hear you and how they can benefit from what you have to say. Imagine something you do well to give you added confidence in yourself. Take several deep breaths and shrug your shoulders prior to being called upon. Repeat your opening words to yourself. Be sure your clothes are neatly arranged so you do not fidget when you are introduced (button your coat).

Focus on your opening line. As you wait to speak, do not think about the content of your speech. Do not worry about your delivery. Instead, focus on how you will start—the first words out of your mouth. At this point, you want to simply bridge the gap of time until you begin, when you will fall into an auto-pilot mode on your previously rehearsed speech. When called, bounce up out of your chair and briskly walk to your position of delivery. Then all systems are go! Your physical enthusiasm will carry through and set the tone for your topic as well as your style.

Don't rush into it. When you reach the podium, do not be in a hurry to start. Many speakers will use a moment before they start to survey the audience and gather their attention for the very first word to be spoken. Let your first words ring loud and clear. Speak loudly enough, as though you were specifically talking to a single individual at the back of the room.

Starting Your Presentation

Remember, you only get one chance to make a first impression. If any portion of your speech has to be exact and sure-fire, it must be your opening. You must initially trust the audience and share with them as though you were speaking to a close friend. You must learn to be intimate with a crowd and like it. If you start your presentation in a casual, informal way, your audience will relax and enjoy your presentation much more than if you start firing facts and figures at them. Your audience must accept you as one of them and as a speaker before they will be willing to listen to and believe what you are saying. But first you must get their attention.

Following are a number of ways that you can grab the attention of your audience and get off to a strong start. Experiment with different types of openings to your presentation to see which works best for you:

State an impressive fact. Grab the attention of the group by telling them something they do not know that is, in some way, surprising. Because people are naturally curious they will want an explanation. Their attention will focus on your next words. "One out of every six people in this room will die of cancer." "The federal government spent more money killing mosquitoes last year than you will earn in your lifetime." "We can double our profit by reducing our expenses within the next two years." With statements like these that are likely to provoke curiosity, you will force audience members to sit up and pay attention.

Tell a joke or story. This has been a traditional method speakers use to warm up the audience. If you are nervous, however, it is usually more difficult to be funny and your nervousness will increase if no one laughs. If you try a joke, be sure it is appropriate and will create a sure-fire laugh; otherwise, try another technique. Also, attempt to make your joke relevant to the situation. Some people are better at telling one-liners and others are better at longer stories. Experiment and see which you prefer. You might be safer to start with a joke that was well received by an audience of which you were a part. Personal stories that relate to the topic are usually effective at drawing the audience into the topic. They are concrete, easy to visualize, and can quickly bring out the importance of the topic. Give an example to further reinforce your introductory statement or thesis of your speech. This can be a personal example or one within the common experience of each audience member. Examples help to clarify and personalize the topic being presented.

Ask a question. Beginning with a rhetorical question will involve the audience as they mentally answer the question for themselves. You can involve them further by asking them to respond to the question by raising their hand. "Let me see the hands of those who would like to know how to more effectively save money." Make sure the question is simple and the audience knows exactly what they are supposed to do. This is a very useful technique to survey the audience quickly, too. For example: "How many people here today watched TV last night?" "How many have watched within the last week?" Information about your audience will help you tailor your material, and the process will involve and interest them at the same time.

Call on a member of the audience. To build rapport with the audience and put everyone at attention, call on an audience member. Choose someone you know or just met and ask a question about the topic of the presentation. At the same time, you will be able to momentarily distract attention from yourself, making the situation less stressful. This technique works better with small audiences

Give a command. Another effective way to physically involve the audience while reducing the attention on you is to tell them to do something. "Before I start, I would like each person to write down one question that he or she would like to have answered in our time together." With this technique, you also increase the probability that individual expectations will be met with your presentation. You can either collect the questions and refer to them toward the end of your speech, or simply ask that each individual be responsible for seeing that the question is answered—either by asking it at an appropriate point in the presentation or at the end of the presentation if the topic was not covered.

Hold up an object. You will engage attention through surprise, interest, or both by holding up an object relevant to your presentation. Plant the object prior to your presentation under the podium or near where you will be standing when you speak.

Be spontaneous. A more advanced technique is to use the first few minutes to say something spontaneous much the same

way we try to build rapport when we first converse with another person. "Can you believe this weather?" or "My spouse told me to be careful today," can serve as appropriate lead-ins to your topic if you tie them into your opening point: "The weather here isn't half as hot as things will be at headquarters if we don't make some changes in our operating plan."—"Although she made the comment in reference to poor driving, I think it has some relevance to my purpose here as well. We need to be careful about the rising accident rate in our regional plants."

Whatever you decide for your attention-getting opening, make sure it is short, simple and sure-fire. It is possible with minimal effort to be able to shift the group's focus from you to the topic and ultimately to how what is being said relates to their own world. Initially, accept the attention and with your opening statements cause the audience to look at the topic with you. Try to be on the same side viewing a mutual problem. As you continue, you will want to answer the questions that audience members have along with the needs, concerns, and objections that they will likely bring up.

Handling the Audience

As you are delivering your presentation pay attention to how effectively you are communicating with your audience. One experienced speaker told me that he thought of speaking as a series of waves. He let his words and feelings roll out over the audience, gave ample time for the meaning to sink in, gauged the reaction and proceeded with the next thought. Another experienced speaker stressed the importance of having the audience come to you, and preferred speaking slowly and quietly so that the audience would be drawn to listen closely. You should try different approaches to find a style with which you are comfortable.

Start with the group. When they are nervous about a presentation, speakers are especially prone to dash off into a topic and leave their audience behind. You need to warm the audience up and give them a few minutes to adjust to you as a person. You need to start slowly and clearly. Most importantly, start to speak in a sensitive manner that indicates that you have an awareness of the significance of the occasion, the topic and the audience. Try to involve the audience either mentally or physically in your opening statements. Listen to the sound of your own voice and react to your message as a member of the audience would.

Never tell your audience that you are uncomfortable or inexperienced at speaking to a group. They want you to do well, and will not favor you starting with excuses as to why you may not do well. Most audiences will have empathy for you anyway, because they know how difficult it can be to speak before a group. They never want to see you fail, because that will make them, as well as you, feel very uncomfortable; and they will not get what they came for.

Enjoy yourself and your audience, even if you despise speaking to them. Be sincerely interested in them as people and in wanting to help them in any way you can. Identify with your audience and focus on how you are like them. Always uplift and inspire them. Make them feel lucky to be in the group. Tell them why your topic is important and how it can help them. Increase your energy level as the size of your group increases. It is often necessary to communicate at a faster pace, as well, to retain the attention of a larger audience.

Involve your audience. Once you have brought your audience to you and set them at ease, and you are all on the same wave length, it is crucial to maintain that link. Converse with them by speaking as if you were exploring a topic together with you serving as spokesperson! Speak from their perspective when possible. Keep them involved and interested with your presentation much the way you would when speaking to only one person. If their attention seems to wane, test to see if you are getting through: ask a question. One or two individuals in a crowd will always drift off or not be interested in what you have to say to begin with, but if that number increases, you need to evaluate the situation and respond.

Does it sound as if you are talking to yourself? Are you getting puzzled or sleepy looks with some people literally scratching their heads? Are others folding their arms and leaning back in their chairs in silent, defensive opposition? If so, you'd best slow down. Stop and ask: "Is this making sense?" or, "I see some puzzled looks...are there any questions?" or, "Let me give you another example to help make that last point a little clearer."

Focus on explaining one point at a time, going from unfamiliar ground to new information. Try to place the members of the audience into the stories and descriptive language. Ask questions the audience might be thinking, such as, "Now you might say..." or "You are probably wondering why...."

You will keep more of the attention of the audience and increase the chances of communicating effectively if you always try to communicate with verbal pictures. If your ideas are abstract, bring them to a more understandable level by giving an example to illustrate the point you are making. For example, it is abstract to speak of percentages when describing an increase in inflation. Instead of quoting only numbers and saying that the rate of inflation had doubled in ten years, say: "Ten years ago, you could by a pastrami sandwich for the amount that today only buys you the bread." Or, instead of using large numbers, when most people cannot imagine above one or two thousand: "The total amount of our profit this year over last year was enough to place $20 into the hands of each employee of the company. That is why we have decided to increase the company's share of medical benefits for all employees." Over 60 percent of what your audience will learn will be through visual communication: from the pictures you create, your nonverbal communication or visual aids.

Keep them on track. If the audience's attention starts to wander, there are a number of ways to retrieve it. You can vary aspects of your voice such as your volume, pitch, and speaking speed. You can change your location in the room, using the movement to recapture their attention. Be sure your movement does not turn into aimless wandering, however, which will be distracting to the group. You can refer to a member of the audience to ask for an opinion on the most recent statement. You can also, as previously described, use an organizational device that is engaging and easy to remember, such as an acronymn made up of the key words of your presentation. During a long presentation, be sensitive to the group's need to take a break. Poll the group at least once very 45 minutes to see if they need to stretch.

Whenever you sense your audience is drifting away or you are losing your momentum, bring them back by saying something like, "This is important because..." or, "What this means for you as employees is...." Bring your topic home to your audience. They want to be led, so lead them.

Always let them know where you are going in your speech. You must use plenty of transition phrases and words such as "next," "now," "put another way," and "in other words." Remember that your audience is not as knowledgeable as you about what you are talking about, and there is no certainty that they care even half as much. They are not listening as closely as you would like them to, so help them out and make it easy for them to identify when you are moving from one point to the next.

You may have to adjust your pace and your speech patterns to suit your audience in order to keep them on your wave length. Politicians are very good at this—they learn to speak only as fast as their audience can understand them, and they don't use big words if they suspect their audience won't understand them.

Since the first and last information from your presentation is more likely to be remembered and stand out, use your best material in the beginning and closing portions of your speech. Give frequent signals as to where you are: "So far we have discussed points one, two and three...and we should now turn our attention to the topic of...." Indicate when you are closing your talk, and audience members will listen more attentively. The summary is a crucial time to restate the key information you want the audience to retain.

Prepare an Emergency Plan

There are several techniques to employ when you are about to lose control of yourself or the audience in a speaking situation. You should envision the worst possible scenario that could take place in your speaking situation and then create a plan for what to do should it actually happen. Possibly, you might be afraid of "going blank" or being unable to continue speaking because of the high level of your anxiety. Having a contingency plan for any circumstances will give you greater confidence and control in the situation. Following are several techniques that you might experiment with and adapt to your own style and situation:

Acknowledge you forgot. As in a conversation, say: "That point momentarily escapes me," and continue on: "But let's look at the other reasons why. . . ."

Fill in the gap. Summarize, repeat the last point, restate your thesis, give a personal example. These tricks will all give you thinking time to remember where you are.

Shift the attention. Ask for questions, poll the group on their opinion or an alternative for what to do next, or take a five-minute break. Remember that no one knows the agenda for your presentation except you!

Refer to your notes. As unobtrusively as possible, glance at your next point. Feel comfortable with the moment or two of silence. Use the silence as a means of letting your thoughts "sink in" or to emphasize your next point.

Summarize and stop. If close to the end of your talk, this might be the best alternative.

Have a catch-all. Practice a line that you will feel comfortable with regardless of the situation. "It seems like I'm getting ahead of myself, let me take a second and catch my breath."

Having diversions planned will keep you from feeling helpless in a moment of panic. It will give you confidence that you have prepared for the worst and have several alternatives from which to choose should the worst happen.

Controlling Physical Symptoms of Stagefright

When we feel the first wave of fear come upon us in a speaking situation, the fear manifests itself in a wide variety of physiological symptoms. These symptoms can cause us to further panic or, at the very least, can distract us or the audience from the presentation.

One of the best ways to control fear is to prevent it from ever gaining a hold on you. There are several methods of controlling the anxiety associated with stagefright. These methods involve first being sensitive to exactly what is happening to your body, and then taking a specific action to counteract the undesired physical reaction. By controlling the symptoms, you will soon be able to "catch" yourself before your fear escalates.

Face Fear Head On

In most cases, your fear and symptoms will pass as you become comfortable in a speaking situation. As you work on your ability to speak and practice in different speaking situations, the duration and intensity of the nervousness and the number of symptoms you experience will diminish. You will feel self-conscious for shorter periods of time when you begin to speak, and learn to shift your attention more quickly to your topic, audience, and purpose.

Instead of trying to hide from your fear, you need to face it squarely. What is the absolute worst that can happen if your presentation fails? What is likely to happen if you do a poor job of speaking to the group? Well, if you were trying to persuade the group to do or buy something, you probably will not. Too bad, but there will be other chances. Their opinion of you might change to include the observation that you are not comfortable when speaking to a group. Again, no permanent damage. You might not receive as large a salary increase for your next performance review. But it is only one factor in that decision, not the sole factor. The point is that fear distorts our perceptions so that it seems like the world will end if we make an error.

What are the chances that your worst fear will occur? Most things we fear are not likely to happen, and likewise the chances that you will totally fail in a speaking situation are small. Even if you do make a mistake, chances are that you will be able to handle the problem so as not to be completely paralyzed in front of the group.

Face it: even if the worst happens to you, very little will change. You won't be fired or demoted. You won't lose friends. You will continue with life as usual. You will go home and have dinner and go to sleep and start the next day as any other. If anyone in the audience had a negative thought about you, your presentation, or your abilities, they will have promptly forgotten it within the hour—if they held it that long. One hundred years from now it will not matter. By this weekend it will not matter. The situation simply should be kept in perspective. This is one of the main lessons to learn in overcoming your fear.

Mentally Relax

There are many mental techniques for controlling stage-fright that are very effective. These techniques can be useful when the fear is more intense prior to or during a presentation.

Mentally escape. Mentally leave the situation by imagining yourself in a different place or time. Think about the last vacation you were on or the next one you plan to take. Think about when you were younger and your life seemed less complicated, or when you will be older and less will matter. Imagine a seaside, the country, or a cabin-with-a-fireplace scene. Try to project yourself there for a few moments.

Imaging. The skill of imaging is similar to that of visualization. (see page 76) It provides you with a means of lessening your fear by associating it with an image and then destroying that image. For example, you can mentally write your worst fears about a speaking situation on helium balloons, and then, one by one, release those balloons in your mind and watch them drift off. If properly done, your fears will float away with the mental image of the balloons. Another example, would be to picture yourself going down an escalator in a tall building. With each level, feel your fear and anxiety level diminishing. By the time you get to the ground floor, be completely free of any fearful thoughts!

Focus on your purpose. Think how important it is for the individuals in your audience to fully understand your message. Think of the benefits they will gain from having learned from your message. Imagine that members of the audience might try to explain your points to others they know. Make your points clear so they can be easily relayed. People who are sincere about and believe in their purpose often are able to come across with greater conviction.

As others sense your sincerity and genuine belief in your own message they become more receptive to it and to you. Enthusiasm is as contagious as sincerity. Your excitement (some of which is actually fear) about the topic and purpose will spread to your audience. As you energize yourself, you will energize your audience.

Focus on a sympathetic listener. To obtain a positive response, one technique many speakers employ is to look for a supportive face in the audience. This can be someone who is smiling, listening intently, or perhaps nodding his or her head in approval of what you are saying. Your attention to such an individual will give you confidence that you are doing a good job in your presentation and thus help to waylay fears and doubts you might start to experience.

Giving yourself suggestions. By encouraging a positive inter-
pretation of your environment and avoiding any negative
reactions to those things happening around you, you can mentally talk to yourself as if you were your own coach. Change
the fabric of your thought. Positive mental suggestions pick
up and amplify stimuli you perceive in your environment
while you are afraid. Some examples: "That person nodded in
agreement to my last sentence—I must be doing well." "This
is easier than I thought it would be; I'm half-way through and
most of the audience still seems very interested in what I am
saying." "I think they like me."

To prevent negative thoughts from setting in, watch out for
internal comments such as: "What a dumb thing to say, I am
making a total fool of myself." Instead, intercept them or immediately follow them with a suggestion to neutralize the comment. "I'm doing well." "They are really interested in what I
have to say . . . I owe it to them to deliver my best." Like water
rolling off a duck's back, let counterproductive thoughts roll
off your psyche: "I am not getting nervous," or "I am starting
to feel tense but it will soon pass. It is not important," or "I am
at peace."

Also, as mentioned earlier, suggestions can be beneficial in
helping you to retain your perspective. "This is only a speech.
All I am doing is talking like I do every day of my life." "It is
not going to make a bit of difference if I do well or mess up.
They will all have completely forgotten who I am in two days
anyway." "Years from now I'll look back and laugh at how
childish I was being about all of this." "Who cares?" Never
take yourself or the situation too seriously.

Physically Relax

Relaxation in stressful situations is a learned behavior for
most of us. We have to consciously be sensitive to our bodies
and minds, and control them both at key times so that they
will not inhibit or immobilize us. Fortunately, most methods

for temporarily discharging tension are relatively simple and easy to learn and practice. Here are a few methods. . .

Breathing. One of the most effective methods of self-control, which is the object of relaxing, is to control your breathing. Breath control can be an art in itself, as evidenced by many disciplines such as yoga. One of the calming exercises that this Eastern practice advocates involves breathing in through one nostril while holding the other closed by placing your index finger against it, holding that breath for eight counts, and then expelling it through the other nostril for four counts. The process is then reversed starting with the other nostril until you have gone through four complete cycles. As you do this, focus on your breathing and let any tension within you drain out as you exhale.

This breathing exercise would be conspicuous if you are before a group, but you can do a similar exercise by simply taking longer, deeper breaths as you start to become anxious. First, fill your stomach region (by use of your diaphragm), then your chest, and finally add an additional volume of air capacity by moving your shoulders up and back. Hold your breath for a moment then slowly expel it, forcibly pushing as much air from your lungs as possible by contracting the muscles in your stomach and chest. If you do this slowly while waiting to speak it is not very noticeable to others. Another breathing technique is forced yawning, in which you start to simulate a yawn so your body will complete it. (See page 00.)

Breath control regulates the amount of oxygen that goes into your blood stream. Whenever you hold your breath or, for example, place your hand over your mouth and nose and attempt to inhale air that you have just exhaled, the amount of oxygen that is available to you in the air is diminished. A lower oxygen level will have the effect of "slowing down" your body processes, which translates into fewer and less prominent symptoms of anxiety and less mental racing of thoughts. It's a way of raising or lowering your body's energy level as you deem appropriate for the situation.

Decubitis. This principle of relaxation states that fatigued muscles will go limp if attention is consciously directed away from them. The principle was first discovered by a person who was bowling and had developed very tired arm muscles from the activity. As he went to pick up the ball after several games, someone called to him and the ball dropped to the floor. Additional experiments found the principle works in a variety of circumstances and the technique began to be used to control muscle tension. The most common forms of relaxing using this approach involve lying down and concentrating on tensing a particular portion of your body, your feet, for example. This tensing will fatigue the muscles in your feet. You then shift your attention to tensing the muscles in your legs. As you do so, the muscles in your feet will relax. You proceed until all muscles in your body have been alternately tensed and relaxed, and then finish by tensing all your muscles at once and totally relaxing. This technique can be easily modified and applied as you are waiting to speak. Alternately tense your arms, legs, neck, etc. while you wait to speak.

Limit visual stimuli. Another popular technique for avoiding panic and hysteria as you stand in front of a group is to limit the amount of visual stimulation you receive. The notion is that speaking before a group is scary because it is visually more intense for the speaker. The maze of faces, each offering nonverbal cues, floods our senses and we are more likely to panic.

Instead of looking out and seeing a blur of faces, look specifically at one face at a time to make speaking before a group more like your day-to-day conversations. Do not move your glance to another face until you have completed your thought. In this way, you will feel as if you are speaking to a series of individuals rather than to a large group. Try to directly catch the glance of every person present before you finish.

You will instantly be able to gain feedback from facial expressions on how you are doing. If you need positive feedback to boost your confidence, simply return to a friendly, supportive face in the group that appears to be enjoying and agreeing with your presentation.

Eye contact is considered to be one of the most effective ways of communicating sincerity. One study indicates 38 percent of all meaning that an audience perceives comes solely from eye contact with individuals in your audience. Avoid looking up or down, or having your eyes dart back and forth. Audiences will typically suspect the speaker is "above them" if he or she refuses to look them in the eyes, and not to be trusted if his or her eyes nervously dart back and forth. Besides, if you are not looking at your audience, you cannot pick up on the crucial feedback you need to know if your message is being communicated.

Handling Specific Symptoms

Here are some more techniques you can have in your hip pocket in the event of an anxiety attack prior to or during your presentation. These methods involve first being sensitive to exactly what is happening in your body, then taking a specific action to counteract the undesired physical reaction.

The symptoms listed are those that are most commonly reported by speakers. For each, tips will be given as to how the symptom can be prepared for and, if possible, how it can be controlled when it occurs. Suggestions will be made, where applicable, for ways you can avoid having these symptoms distract from your delivery.

THE ANNOYING SYMPTOMS

Rocking body movements. Excessive body movements are an outlet for nervous energy. Any type of mannerism can be distracting and so should be avoided. Focus on keeping your weight on the balls of your feet and having your body be "dead" from the waist down. Planting your feet in this manner when you start speaking will encourage nervous movements to be translated into upper body gestures. Likewise, this stance will help to keep you from leaning on a podium too much if one is present. If your hands feel awkward and unnatural at your side, try placing one in your pocket and holding the other bent in front of you. This stance is better than gripping a lectern that is in front of you or clutching a note pad.

Shaky muscles. Shaky muscles may show up as trembling hands or wobbly knees. The harder you try to control these muscles, the more they tend to shake. Once you isolate the tension, however, there are a number of ways to remove it. It is often effective to "shake off" the energy in tense muscles, particularly in the case of those tell-tale hands, arms and legs. Shake your limbs vigorously before you enter the room in which you will be speaking, or walk around briskly. Consciously tensing specific muscles as hard as possible and then quickly relaxing your control is another effective method of removing tension. The key is to move the tense muscles.

Do not let your presentation make your shaking more apparent. If your hands are shaky, do not hold up any visual aids or point to items on a board or overhead projector. Likewise, if your knees are shaky, you may want to initially start speaking while leaning against or sitting on the edge of a table, if possible. Do not feel you are locked into having to speak from one specific location, even if a podium is present. I've even seen a speaker at a conference speak to the audience from a chair next to the podium!

Twitches and mannerisms. Irregular muscle spasms or mannerisms can be difficult to control, but at the very least, be aware of them so that you can try different ways to stop them. Rubbing the area, as in a twitch over an eye, may help. Turning that side of your body or face away from the audience may help you to make it less conspicuous. Be on guard to catch other mannerisms, such as playing with a pen or pencil. Ask a friend in the audience to watch for them as well and devise a method so that he or she can signal to you to stop an annoying mannerism.

Loose change. Hands in the pockets can be annoying to an audience if you are playing with change or keys. It also restricts the use of the arm gestures and so is apt to make you less effective than you could be. If you have the tendency to jingle loose change, use a change purse or be sure that the pocket is empty.

Cracking voice. If your body is extremely tense, your voice is likely to give you away. The voice is a marvelously sensitive barometer of our feelings—you must learn to make it work for you, not against you. It is difficult to effectively change or control your voice, but it is possible. The problem usually comes from having tense neck muscles or an inadequate air supply to support your voice. Stretch your neck, roll your head, clear your throat, have a drink of water, and take a deep breath to counteract the effects of this symptom.

"Ahs" and "umms." Possibly one of the most difficult mannerisms to correct is the verbal crutch of saying "ah" during a pause in your speech. When excessive, these faults can distract an audience and so should be avoided. Practice speaking more deliberately with intentional pauses, always thinking before you speak. Practice stopping and learn to be comfortable with silence. Listen to your own voice so as to be aware of any sloppy use of language. Sometimes, verbal fillers are a sign that you have not prepared enough. Go over your presentation out loud and if that is not adequate to stop the problem, write your speech out, memorizing it, if necessary. Once you overcome this verbal crutch, you can then return to a more informal mode of delivery which is usually considered more effective and appropriate.

THE DECELERATION SYMPTOMS

Shortness of breath. Not having enough air to finish a sentence and not being able to take a complete breath are both caused by excessive muscle tension around your chest and stomach regions. There are a number of tricks to keep you loose prior to your presentation. A deep breath with a stretching of the arms will help to break the chest tension and, at the same time, give you maximum air volume. If you are unable to take a full, long breath, focus your energy on exhaling as completely as possible. The inhaling will come more naturally. Another trick is to make yourself yawn. You do this by inhaling a series of consecutive, short breaths, almost as if your lungs were a balloon that you were filling with air. If you are unable to create a yawn at will, pay attention to what you physically feel the next time your body has a natural yawn. With practice you can then recreate the sensation at will. Naturally, you get all of this out of your system before you go in front of the group.

If you find you have or are becoming short of breath while speaking, simply stop and take a deep breath. Take a moment between sentences or phrases to catch your breath and re-establish a natural speaking rhythm. If you don't stop and dissipate your tension, you will be apt to breathe shallower and shallower as you keep talking. This will cause you to break sentences with unnatural pauses and make what you are saying more difficult to understand.

Pausing to take a deep breath will allow you time to think about what you want to say next. The audience will forgive you for stopping to collect your thoughts. If you feel uncomfortable stopping, give your audience a disclaimer such as: "Let me take a second and catch my breath, I'm starting to get ahead of myself." Most likely, you will come across as being very excited about your topic, which can be very positive.

Dry mouth. The reaction opposite of excessive sweating is dehydrating. Dry or "cotton mouth" can be uncomfortable and will affect your ability to pronounce words and speak clearly. If you are prone to this symptom, have a glass of water handy or request one while you are speaking.

Stiff muscles. This is a physiological symptom that is a carry-over from our primitive "fight or flight" instinct. Remember, the mind does not distinguish between real and imagined fear; the body gets the same instructions either way. Our muscles are tensed and prepared for action. When muscles are extremely tense they start to shake, just as your arm shakes when you try to squeeze an object very hard. Stiff muscles can cause a very rigid and animated delivery. They can hamper your ability to speak, as in a "white knuckle" gripping of the podium. Muscle tension may only be displayed in one or two symptoms, but the tension runs throughout your system, affecting the vocal and respiratory muscles.

Learn to identify exactly which muscles are the most tense. These are the sets of muscles where your tension is focused and you can identify a distinct manifestation of tension. Identifying tense muscles may not be an easy thing to do. Your mind is on many other things while you are in a speaking situation and you will have to pause to think about where the tension is in your body. Move the muscles that are tight. For example, a stiff front torso can often be relaxed by bending at the waist, perhaps to pick up an object, to "break" the rigid body armor prior to speaking.

THE ACCELERATION SYMPTOMS

Racing. If your reaction to fear is to become progressively more excited you can again control your response. If your heart is pounding and your head is swimming, pause, close your eyes and take a deep breath. Your intent is to try to limit the stimuli that are overexciting you. Imagine a peaceful scene or a favorite pastime. Stopping and redirecting your thoughts will redirect your behavioral response as well.

Pounding heart. This symptom is your body's way of preparing you for quick, defensive action. We seldom need this "fight or flight" energy today, although the extra energy can help us to be mentally alert. The pounding sound in our ears can be distracting to us, but, of course, cannot be heard by anyone else. Taking long, slow breaths prior to and during a presentation when you get a rush of anxiety will help to slow your heart down. In extreme cases, holding a long, deep breath will decrease the amount of oxygen available to your blood and slow down your pounding heart.

Fast talking. Many people vent their nervousness in speaking situations by talking faster and faster. Although we are able to comprehend up to four or five times faster than the typical speaker speaks, "shotgunning" information in a steady stream of verbiage with minimal inflection is bothersome to listen to for most audiences. This symptom can be controlled by learning to pause and pace yourself; by being comfortable with silence. Techniques to try to achieve this comfort include using sparse notes such as the reminder "SLOW DOWN" written in the margin. If you know someone in the audience, you can ask him or her before the meeting to give you some type of signal if you begin to speak too quickly. Or, at the very least, practice saying the most important information of your talk (key points and transitions; opening and closing sentences) louder, slower and more clearly. A varied pace is easier to listen to and to understand.

Excessive sweating. Getting flushed or warm because of anxiety often makes people sweat excessively. This visible sweat on forehead, around the neck, in the palm of the hands or from the armpits is beyond your control. The less you worry about it, the better it will be. However, you can minimize the embarrassment by planning ahead. Have a handkerchief available and don't be shy about mopping your brow. Your audience will understand; after all, aren't you working very hard on their behalf? Loosen your collar if it is tight prior to speaking and, if you wear glasses, dab some cornstarch on the nose bridge to avoid slippage. Wear a white shirt or blouse if you are prone to have wet underarms or simply do not remove your jacket. To cool down, drink some water. You can usually make sure that a glass of cool water is near the podium prior to the group arriving or bring a glass up with you when you begin to speak. In extreme cases, you may develop a rash. These symptoms will go away when the perceived threat of speaking is over, and will be less likely to occur as you gain comfort with speaking.

THE HALTING SYMPTOMS

Mental block. Extreme fear is usually associated with an unwillingness to even consider the possibility of doing that which is dreaded. We "block out" thinking about the task and procrastinate to keep from adequately preparing. We can't even start to think about speaking. If this occurs to you, focus energy on small, preliminary steps in preparation of your presentation. Focus, for example, on your topic selection and organization rather than wasting time simply dreading the upcoming experience and worrying about negative consequences.

Blanking out. One of the most extreme responses we can experience during delivery of a presentation is paralysis in front of a group. We forget what we are saying or were going to say or even what we just said. This dreaded symptom can devastate most speakers, yet a similar occurrence often happens when we forget what we were saying in a typical conversation. When speaking with just one other person, we seldom are devastated when we lose our train of thought. It is quite natural to simply say, "What was I saying?" Or, if the group is too large for you to ask for or obtain assistance from anyone, simply continue with another point that strikes you as being important at the time: "That example will come to me, but meanwhile, one point I haven't emphasized is . . . ." The extra moment that either of these alternatives provides can be a pause, not an embarrassing silence, if you don't chastise yourself.

Speechlessness. Another form of blanking out is not being able to speak at all. Warm up your voice prior to entering a speaking environment and perhaps even hum softly to yourself while you are waiting to start. Repeat the first words you plan to say to yourself. If you become speechless in the middle of your talk, stop and accept the feeling, take a breath and then begin. Focus on the face of a friend in the audience and speak as if you are talking to just one person. If absolutely nothing comes out of your mouth, at least force a laugh. This will put your audience at ease and serve as a mutual release, since they are not likely to want you to fail.

Headaches. When allowed to develop, headaches can debilitate a speaker. Any physical symptom prior to, during, or after a presentation is most likely a direct result of excessive tension. For example, one type of headache is caused by having your back and neck muscles tighten so much that your scalp is pulled taut, resulting in forehead pain from the pressure. Another common speaking headache occurs from not eating earlier in the day because you had no appetite due to anxiety. In the former case, take some aspirin hours before your presentation on a preventative basis; in the latter case, eat something, however little, such as a bag of peanuts, to give your body needed energy.

Drugs for Stagefright Symptoms

In the last few years a drug marketed in the U.S. under the name Inderal (generic: propranolol) has been used in a number of studies of people with extreme cases of anxiety or stagefright.

Inderal is one of a class of drugs known as beta-blockers, meaning that it interferes with the nervous stimulation of the cardiovascular system by blocking the beta receptors on cells. It eliminates the physical manifestations of stagefright—the racing heart, tremors and excessive sweating—without depressing mental functioning as is more common with other drugs such as Valium. While typically prescribed only for people with certain heart conditions and high blood pressure, Inderal has also been found to reduce some of the physical symptoms of severe anxiety.

Inderal is not a cure-all, however. It is a powerful, prescription-only drug. The dosage required for reducing the symptoms of stagefright is very small and, at present, its use for stagefright is limited. Inderal might be considered for someone with a history of being unable to control his or her stagefright symptoms, and for whom presentations or performances are a required and regular part of a career. Whether Inderal will be used on a widespread basis for the symptomatic treatment for stagefright symptoms is not yet clear.

Inderal can also have serious side effects. It can be dangerous for people with asthma, hay fever, bronchitis, and some types of diabetes and heart conditions. It can cause dizziness or drowsiness, cold hands and feet, loss of appetite, loss of hair, and fatigue.

If you are one of those who suffers from serious anxiety and nervous physical symptoms when speaking in public, you might consult your physician about Inderal. A more practical solution for most people, however, is simply to have an alcoholic drink before speaking, perhaps a glass of wine at lunch, if you are speaking in the afternoon. Besides relaxing you, alcohol slightly deadens your nerves and senses, thereby decreasing the amount of perceptual input you receive. You will be less overwhelmed by the situation and less likely to panic. Of course, if you are not careful, and you have too many drinks, your ability and control will suffer. To make a successful presentation you cannot slur your speech or stumble on the way to the front of the room! Set a one- or two-drink maximum for yourself.

The Fear Map Revisited

The Fear Map was used earlier as a means of evaluating your comfort levels with certain variables that affect any presentation you might make. The Fear Map can also be used to evaluate how prepared you are for a specific speaking engagement.

First, go through the analysis and answer all of the questions with the specific speaking situation in mind. Plot the levels on the map. Second, answer all the questions from the perspective of how prepared you believe you currently are for handling this specific speaking task. Again, plot your answer. The graphic difference between the two plots will represent the degree of your "relative readiness." If the gap is large, your relative readiness is small; you might be better off to decline the engagement or plan to prepare more. If you do go ahead, this analysis can help determine where you most need to spend your preparation time in order to narrow the dimension gaps and to feel confident enough for the presentation.

Following are some other tips for speaking, categorized by the four sectors of the Fear Map: the topic, the audience, the situation, and the speaker.

THE TOPIC

• **Complexity**. If your topic seems too complex or abstract, clarify it by adding examples or increasing the avenues of communication, for instance use a handout *plus* overhead slides *plus* two-way discussion. (See page 99 in the appendix for suggestions on preparing visual aids.)

• **Familiarity**. Don't accept a topic for presentation unless you know approximately half of what you will say at the time of acceptance (a rule many speakers use). Have a friend quiz you on the topic prior to your talk.

• **Purpose**. Scale your purpose to the level of the audience. If you don't think you can persuade the audience, try just to inform them of a different perspective. Survey them during your presentation, prior to your presentation, or when you first start to speak to measure where they currently stand on your topic.

THE AUDIENCE

• **Group size**. If you are intimidated by the size of a group, try looking just over their heads as you deliver your talk. As you gain comfort, look at individual pairs of eyes in the group.

• **Expertise**. If someone in the audience seems to know more on an issue than you, invite them to share their information with the group. Flatter or compliment the group, saying such things as "As you probably know...."

• **Disposition**. Try to meet each member of the audience, or as many as possible, prior to a presentation. Shake hands; the physical contact breaks down mental distance and builds trust. Minimize the degree of evaluation by speaking with anyone who appears to be judging you during a break or calling on that person during the talk. Pick on the largest person in the room to jibe in a mild way.

THE SITUATION

- **Timing**. Jot down three points you want the audience to remember. Do an outline of your entire presentation in five minutes. Pretend you have half the time to prepare that you really do; set a deadline for your halfway mark.

- **Formality**. If you are more comfortable being informal in a group, say so and do what is necessary to become loose, including: taking off your jacket, sitting while talking, or asking the group questions about the topic.

- **Environment**. Good speakers take control of the speaking environment by doing something no one else in the room has the situational authority to do, as in: asking someone to do something (turn a light on or off, fetch some supplies, move furniture), asking a question, or stating guidelines for your task.

THE SPEAKER

- **Ability**. Strive to speak frequently in front of a group, at least one or two times a week. Use work and social settings.

- **Motivation**. Build positive consequences for doing well by promising yourself a reward. Track your progress to gain momentum.

• **Commitment.** Make a time commitment to adequately prepare. Block out time on your calendar. Talk about your presentation with friends, your manager, and/or your spouse. Tell them what you plan to say and get their reactions and suggestions. Volunteer when possible for a speaking situation to avoid feeling "trapped" or forced into speaking.

Handling Questions Without Panic

Often time will be allowed after your presentation for the audience to ask questions. This question-and-answer time causes anxiety for many speakers who feel they may be asked a question that they will be unable to answer or be put on the spot by a hostile member of the audience. Fortunately, almost all questions you will be asked can be predicted in advance of your presentation, and researching for the answers is an important part of your preparation (see pages 95 and 107 in the appendix). Think through who will be the typical (or better yet, the specific) members of the audience, and what concerns they are likely to have. Try to figure out the most difficult or embarrassing questions they might come up with. Obtain questions from individuals with whom you practice your presentation.

If there are questions or objections that you are almost certain will be raised, you should consider bringing up the concern in your presentation. For example: "Now I know a lot of you are probably thinking, 'If this is such a great idea, why haven't we done it before' and my answer to that is, 'We've never had as good an opportunity as we do today.'"

In addition to predicting questions you will be asked, you will have less anxiety if you have a plan for *how* you will answer questions. Following are some techniques you should consider incorporating into your own method of answering questions:

1. **Repeat the question.** This allows you a chance to organize your thoughts and make sure you clearly understand the questions. It is also a courtesy to those members of the audience who may not have heard the question.

2. **Compliment good or tough questions.** Saying "that's an excellent question, I'm glad you brought it up" will flatter the questioner and make it easier for you both to arrive at an acceptable answer. By selectively complimenting questions you can also help to direct attention to the points you wish to reinforce in your presentation. Do not compliment every question or you will seem insincere.

3. **"Frame" the answer, if necessary.** Give background information, relevant factors or assumptions if needed to support your answer or make it clear to all audience members. "Your question assumes that I am not interested in a timely resolution to the problem when in fact that is one of my highest priorities."

4. **Answer the question clearly.** If you give a long answer make sure you specifically have answered the stated question. Some speakers give a short answer first and then elaborate on the question. "To answer your question, I do not believe we should bring in an outside consultant for this problem, and let me tell you specifically why not. . . ."

5. **Check the clearness of your answer.** If there is any doubt, ask if your response clearly answers the individual's question. If the individual disagrees with your answer and proceeds to debate the issue, ask to speak with him or her in greater depth after the group breaks up or simply take another question.

6. **Have a plan for questions you can't answer.** If you get a question you are unprepared for, it is usually better to admit you don't have an answer than to bluff a response. Offer to get

back to the individual, refer to someone present who might have a suitable answer, or turn the question back on the individual or audience in general: "I don't have an answer to that question; I'll do my best to obtain the information and contact you as soon as I do." Or, "I really am not prepared to answer your question; can anyone else here help us out?"

7. **Be prepared for hostile questions.** Although it is seldom that an audience member will be openly hostile to your presentation, if you are prepared for such a person you'll be all the more confident. You should attempt to diffuse the hostility so the question can be handled objectively. Recognizing the emotion or stating that there may be disagreement about the topic is one way to diffuse hostility. "From your question I can tell that you disagree with my proposal, but let me return to the facts. . . ." Focusing on those points on which you and the hostile audience member agree is another effective technique for averting hostile emotions. "You agree with me, then, on several points—namely. . . ." If you are able to do so appropriately, humor will go a long way toward releasing tension in the speaking situation. Be certain to be professional and stay on the topic and the points made by the hostile audience member. Never attack the individual personally even if that individual has made a personal slur against you. Your audience will think less of you if you do.

III. After the Applause

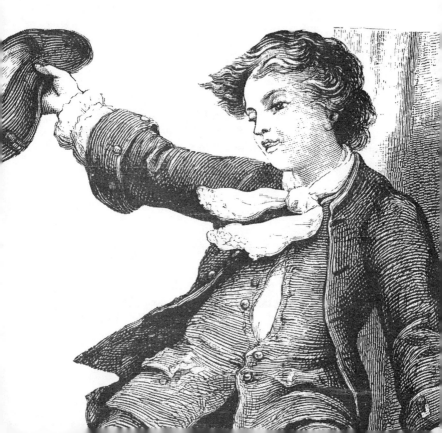

If you've come along this far in the book, you will no doubt have picked up a few tricks and techniques to help you cope with stagefright. You also are likely to have a better understanding of what you fear and why, and have been able to raise your level of comfort in speaking to groups.

Unfortunately, many individuals who are faced with an upcoming speaking situation do not have the time to break in a new habit prior to their first engagement. If this is the case, it is all the more important to take that time after your first presentation to learn and develop your skills to be ready for next time. Keep the first occasion in perspective and do not expect too much of yourself, but be committed to address the problem in more detail at a later time. In this chapter, the focus is on long-range solutions to stagefright. It includes skills that might take time to learn and master but that will raise your confidence to higher levels and thus give you even greater comfort in speaking situations. Developing these skills can help you reach a point where you welcome being in the limelight because you have permanently overcome your fear of speaking.

Additional Skills for Overcoming Stagefright

Usually when we think about what skills are needed to be an effective speaker, we come up with a standard list that describes a good speaker we have heard. We might have been attracted to their "presence" and considered them to be dynamic, interesting speakers. Or, we might have been awed by their ability to handle the mechanics of speaking: the strength, clarity and inflection of their voices or their ability to weave words and phrases and come across in a very organized professional manner. Although these are all excellent attributes for any speaker —and ones we can all hope to acquire—they may be of little value to the speaker who has stagefright. Instead, there are other skills—mental skills—that may prove easier to master and invaluable for overcoming speaking fears.

Such intangible skills as imagination, concentration, memory retention, and visualization probably are as important to overcoming stagefright and becoming an effective speaker as are the traditional skills associated with speaking to groups, such as voice control and humor. These skills will be valuable both prior to and during the delivery of your presentation. They are easy to learn and simply require a willingness to try them coupled with a change of attitude about their importance. Here is a description of the skills and how they can help you overcome your fear so you can speak in front of groups with greater ease:

Imagination

Imagination may not seem like a speaking skill at all, but it is very valuable in many speaking situations. Imagination is a mentally stretching and expanding process whereas fear tends to be a retreating, defensive behavior. It is useful for identifying interesting topics and developing them prior to speaking engagements. It is useful for thinking through consequences of future behavior, such as determining what questions are apt to be asked or what would be the worst situation that could arise during your presentation. This will give you a jump on preparing for future possibilities. Imagination is also valuable for naturally and spontaneously inserting fresh ideas and perspectives into your speaking; for describing information or "painting a picture" to a group; or using analogies. Mental brainstorming will usually provide exciting opportunities for you to alter your attitude and approach to speaking.

How do you develop your imagination? For preparation purposes try thinking in terms of extremes: What can I tell this group that they have probably never heard before? What are all the possible ways of beginning my speech? How can I take a commonly held belief and show that it is false? Then, evaluate the consequences of those extremes. What is keeping you from trying that extreme approach? If you are very creative, your scenarios and ideas might need to be toned down.

You can also use your imagination while you are speaking. Some speakers imagine the entire group is in their underwear to help them keep their perspective. Others pretend they are speaking to a board of directors to give importance to their purpose and deliberateness to their manner.

Organization

If you learn to become more organized about your presentations, much of your anxiety associated with speaking to groups will fade away. When preparing a presentation, being organized will help you to structure your message and see what information you need to research prior to your delivery. Better organization will mean less chance of confusion during your delivery.

An organized person would block out time to prepare and practice a presentation far enough in advance to avoid panic. An organized person would also select appropriate visual aids to support his or her message and style and develop those aids far enough in advance of the presentation (see page 99 in the appendix, Using Visual Aids).

To become more organized, make this trait a high priority. Be systematic in the way you prepare and practice your presentations. Make lists and check off items as they are completed. Keep related notes or materials together with staples,

paper clips, or rubber bands, or keep them in labeled boxes. Buy a file cabinet and manila folders to keep your materials logically categorized and in order.

Concentration

Perhaps the opposite of imagination, concentration involves focusing your energy and maintaining that focus on a single item. This is another essential skill to develop to be effective at overcoming speaking fears. The ability to concentrate will help you keep from procrastinating when you need to prepare. It will also help give you confidence so that you can deliver a strong opening to a speech regardless of your fears. It can help keep you from being distracted during your delivery,and help keep you calm when you feel you are losing control.

You can best learn how to concentrate at times when you least want to do it. When you are tired, practice focusing your thoughts; when you feel emotional, try to minimize the display of those emotions; when you have forgotten a bit of information, work on systematically recreating the sequence of events or circumstances that led you to learning that bit of information to begin with. Prior to beginning a speech, repeat the first words of your talk over and over to yourself so you will be confident they are there when you start. Focus on making positive remarks to yourself when you do not feel positive.

Greater concentration will be required as the speaking situation seems more difficult for you; just as driving a car at 70 mph requires greater concentration than driving it at 30 mph. You also need to be able to easily switch your attention from your material to your audience and assess the reactions of your listeners. Some speakers refer to this concept as "moving the anchor of awareness." Try to keep your focus off yourself and away from other mental or physical distractions. This can easily be done if you make sure that what you are saying or how you are saying it will hold the attention of the group.

Visualization

Of the mental skills discussed so far, visualization will be the most useful in allowing you to gain comfort with speaking. One of the fundamental qualities of fear that gives it its strength is its unknown nature. We are either not sure what to expect when we face a speaking situation, or are afraid something worse than we have previously experienced will occur. The ability to visualize will eliminate many of the unknowns we fear in speaking situations. It will, in addition, be a valuable skill in relating information to a group in a clear, interesting manner.

To use visualization to reduce fear, mentally picture yourself in the speaking situation that you fear. First, picture yourself in the empty room (and if you can actually visit the room prior to speaking, by all means do so). Then, visualize yourself at the front of the empty room standing by a podium. Next, imagine yourself talking in front of this empty room. You might want to stand wherever you are now and pretend you are speaking to the audience. Speak first to a small audience, then to a larger one, up to the expected size of the group. Mentally walk through this sequence several times.

Visualization, or communicating "pictures," is also one of the most effective means of relating information to a group. When you speak to groups, try as frequently as possible to describe images. This technique will help make your message easier to comprehend and much more interesting. It also has the advantage of giving you a great deal of flexibility in organizing your information because of the many ways that a picture can be described. If you missed a detail, simply go on to state it, and no one will know that it had been left out. In fact, a point speakers sometimes forget is that the audience does not know what your outline or agenda for speaking is. Communicating a picture can make explaining an abstract idea much easier because the audience has a tangible base upon which to build.

Stories and examples are prime uses of visualization. Audiences naturally perk up and listen more closely when a story is being told. When you communicate a picture, you will have much more information about a set of circumstances than is ever explicitly stated. It is our natural tendency to fill in any gaps of a mental picture with what our past experience has told us to expect of the situation. In this regard you will have the audience playing a more active role in understanding your message.

Memory Retention

If you have confidence in your memory, you will never worry about "blanking out" or losing your place in your speech. In speaking, you need to trust your memory to produce several bits of information with a minimum amount of prodding. You need to be able to look at a few words jotted on a note card and from them recall a wealth of details. A good memory is also an asset in answering questions.

One of the first steps in building good memory skills is to

know from your own past experience what you are most likely to forget. Then, devise ways that will keep you from forgetting. One effective strategy for organizing information in a way that will increase the likelihood of remembering is to insert a mental hint with the information you want to remember. For example: if you want to remember the five reasons the union went on strike in the company's Pennsylvania plant last year, you could prompt yourself by associating each of the reasons with fictitious characters who work at the plant: Mr. Insurance, Miss Days, Mr. Overtime, etc. By planting hints that are easier to remember, you can jog your memory.

Another memory building technique is to associate the new information you want to remember within the context of something you are unlikely to forget. You could create an acronym using the first letters of words, phrases or points you want to remember. In the example above, you could use the P-L-A-N-T sequence to trigger key words, thoughts or relationships: Performance reviews, Last contract, Absenteeism, New insurance, Time-and-a-half.

It is also possible to develop a lower reliance on notes. Notes are considered appropriate in most prepared speaking situations, but should not serve as a crutch. Practice writing out a complete thought, then try to deliver that thought from a three-word phrase, and then from a single key word. See how close you can come to stating the original thought when you just look at the key word several days later.

Four Additional Approaches

There are a host of theories and approaches that have been successfully used in overcoming stagefright. This book has so far advocated a practical, systematic approach using the Fear Map. You may want to try some additional approaches that have been successfully used to help those who have speaking fears. These include the rational emotive theory; systematic desensitization; awareness—acceptance—action; and hypno-therapy.

Rational Emotive Theory

This theory, first developed by Robert Ellis, states, in a sim-plified form, that we are able to control our emotions, includ-ing fear and anxiety, through our thoughts. We can rationally redefine our reality for ourselves by first changing the way we think about our fear. As applied to the fear of speaking, this theory would consist of the following four steps:

1. Imagination. Imagine the worst that could happen in your speaking situation. Take your analysis to an extreme. Perhaps it might be the audience criticizing you or even outright laugh-ing at you. Or maybe they will be so disgusted by your delivery that they will start to ignore you or leave the room. Your manager might become so outraged that he fires you—in front of the group! You might become so stressed that you have a heart attack and die on the spot!!!

2. Probablity. Now, of the negative consequences that could occur as a result of your presentation, what are the chances that any or all of them will actually materialize? For most negative consequences, especially as they become extreme, the chances of them occurring become very small.

3. Visualization. With the negative consequences no longer being an unknown intangible, picture what is more likely to occur in your speaking situation and what specific problems might realistically arise.

4. Action. Decide to act to minimize the chances of not being able to handle the specific problems you identified that might arise. Resolve to not worry about those aspects of the situa-tion over which you have no control.

This theory helps to change "blind" fear into a more tangible set of potential negative consequences, with a probability of occurrence for each. It is a means of converting an irrational, emotional feeling into a rational process that can be examined and discussed. By doing so, the mystery of the unknown disappears and energy can be directed toward those specific ends where it will do the most good.

Systematic Desensitization

This process also makes use of the speaker's imagination in confronting the fear of speaking. It has proven to be one of the more effective methods for those experiencing extreme anxiety over presentational speaking.

With this method, the individual shuts his or her eyes and attempts to mentally walk through the stressful situation from its earliest conception to its final completion. Whenever stress is felt, the individual stops the exercise and simply attempts it again after the anxiety has subsided. No analysis is made as to why the fear exists or why it goes away. The mental exercise is repeated until the individual is able to mentally "walk through" the entire speaking situation from start to finish without experiencing any physical anxiety.

A different approach which makes use of the same theory involves learning to face other intangible fears. Practice controlling your fright in situations where you know that there is no physical harm that can come to you. A good example is watching a scary movie. You know that the threat is imagined, yet the symptoms you experience are very real. It serves as an ideal situation to face your fear in order to be better able to work with it.

Go to a scary movie and, as you are watching, become aware of what your body is doing. Are you squirming? Sit erect, facing the screen full front. Is your heart pounding? Close your eyes and consciously take longer and deeper breaths. Continue breathing in this deliberate manner as you watch. Experiment with giving yourself suggestions. "This is not that scary." "This is only a movie." "I am completely relaxed." "The music is scarier than the visual." See which suggestions are most effective in diminishing your symptoms of fear and remember them for use later in those "fearful nightmares" of public speaking.

By doing this type of exercise, you are learning how to control irrational feelings in a rational way. You are using your ability to think, to anticipate and overpower your emotions when they are not serving constructive purposes. Many times we do not want to control our emotions. For example, when we are angry and feel we have a right to be angry, we may prefer to vent and display that anger. It is still a valuable skill, however, to know how to avoid or contain our anger in situations in which we deem it inappropriate. Establish the point at which fear becomes counterproductive for you if left unchecked. Learn how to contain or diminish fear below that level.

If you recognize your fear and learn to accept it, you can bring it to controllable levels. Instead of being scared into paralysis or inappropriate behavior, you will simply become nervous about speaking situations. That level, which is more manageable, will serve to assist you in your progress towards becoming an effective speaker.

You can learn to face your fear. Find those speaking situations that are least fearful and practice being bolder and bolder. Slowly move toward more threatening situations as your comfort level increases. Most people find that speaking situations they volunteer for are somehow less of a threat than those in which they have no choice about speaking. In part, this is because they have, and have accepted, greater control. Practice on groups in which consequences of poor performance will be less devastating to you or your career. In any situation, if you choose, you can prepare for the worst that could happen.

Awareness—Acceptance—Action

This technique involves a simple formula that many people use in coping with different fears. It involves being *aware* of the fear, *accepting* the fear as being valid, and *acting* on the fear.

1. **Awareness.** Be sensitive to what is happening to you when you become fearful. Once you are sensitized to your level of fear, you will be better equipped to stop the escalation of your fear. Even panic, which often occurs instantaneously, can be more effectively curtailed when you recognize what is happening to you. Start paying attention to the physical changes that occur within your body when you begin to fear something. Notice your breathing pattern, muscle tension and other symptoms that will tell how nervous or relaxed you are feeling.

2. **Acceptance.** Once you are able to sense when you are scared, you need to learn to accept the emotion as being valid and quit feeling guilty, foolish or inferior because of it. It is perfectly natural to be anxious in speaking situations. In fact, to not be "on edge" about a presentation is unnatural even for experienced speakers. To deny that this nervousness is normal, or say that it should not be happening, is going to make you more fearful and less likely to be able to handle your fear. Instead, when fear comes, welcome it! Consider it a form of energy that can motivate you to better prepare prior to a presentation and make you a more enthusiastic speaker during your delivery. *Treat your fear as an ally that can make you a better speaker.*

3. **Action.** After you are aware of and accept fear, you need to act upon it. Do something different! Do not become a passive recipient of a feeling you dread. At first, you might try any different behavior such as changing your breathing pattern or laughing. With some experience, you will be able to identify more specifically what action curtails your fear. If you do not

take aggressive action to counter your fear, it is apt to grow and paralyze you. If you simply stand there as you feel fear set in, you will be increasingly uncomfortable. Your seemingly automatic response will take over and a feeling of panic will escalate. The longer you wait, the less you will be able to combat the emotion.

Hypnotherapy

Another known "cure" that can be employed to overcome stagefright is hypnosis. Although this might seem like a mysterious and magical solution, for the most part, hypnosis is very practical. In fact, hypnosis is credited with being one of the most effective methods for reducing stagefright. This method will typically combine visual imagery and self-suggestions. After specifically identifying what an individual fears in a speaking situation, suggestions are designed either by you or in conjunction with a hypnotist to help in overcoming anxiety. These suggestions might consist of affirmations or other positive statements that would boost the confidence of the speaker or serve as reminders of specific alternatives that are available to the individual in lieu of becoming anxious. With repetition over several weeks, usually with the aid of a tape recorder, the subject integrates the new suggestions into his or her mental and behavioral responses to speaking situations. Hypnosis is also possible without the aid of a hypnotist. Several books are available on the topic of self-hypnosis and self-suggestion.

These methods just described represent the most effective techniques known for overcoming stagefright in presentational speaking situations. Through them you can become skilled at managing your level of anxiety and redirecting the normal surge of energy that comes with speaking into channels that enhance rather than detract from your presentation. Arm gestures, body motion and enthusiasm can become the acceptable outlets for your nervous energy that will, in addition, improve your presentation's effectiveness.

Permanently Overcoming Stagefright

All real growth is accompanied by a feeling of discomfort and challenge. Any new behavior is going to feel awkward at first. In order for change to occur on a permanent basis, you must want to make a change, and then follow through by actually doing something differently. To make the change permanent, you must reinforce the new behavior internally and externally as soon as possible and for an extended period of time.

Maintaining Your Commitment

If you have the commitment to change and the courage and patience to go through a period of uneasiness as you learn new behaviors, you will conquer your fear. The more you venture into new speaking situations, and the greater the frequency of your speaking, the faster you will progress. The faster you change your way of thinking about speaking, the sooner you will display new ways to react to your fear. Mentally learning to become comfortable with risk, or redefining what situations are risky to you, will help you to become unafraid of being embarrassed in front of a group. Visualize yourself "hamming it up" in front of others and you will come to enjoy the chance to speak, rather than seriously dread the opportunity as another chance to fail.

Like a smallpox vaccination, you need to be exposed to small doses of fear in order to be prepared against a major exposure which can paralyze you. The process of striving to improve must continue as you become comfortable with speaking to groups so that you do not regress into previous patterns of fear behavior. Do not feel only a sense of relief that you are done with a presentation and then promptly forget about speaking until the next situation becomes imminent. To do so will place you on a treadmill of fear—always facing the same fear each time. (This is especially true if your speaking occasions are infrequent and all you remember from the last engagement is the dread that you felt before, during and even perhaps after you spoke.) Instead, make speaking a vital part of your life, a part you seek out and look forward to.

Although you may have heard that stagefright is something that one never gets over, I strongly disagree. You can and will come to control the situations that you are fearful in, and the doubt and fear you experience in speaking situations will diminish. Your comfort level will increase with each experience if you are doing the right things to reinforce new behaviors. Your confidence will spread to new speaking situations such as larger groups or different types of audiences. Most people will continue to experience at least some form of "butterflies," which is, as has been discussed, probably for the best.

The Comfort of Habit

After you have experienced a new behavior a few times, it will begin to feel more comfortable. Soon you may even forget what the old behavior was like and only have positive behavioral choices to select from. If you do nothing else, the sheer number of times you speak will cause you to become more comfortable with this activity. It will give you more chances to experiment with behavior and material that works for you with an audience. Try to speak every week before a group to keep your skills tuned and your fear at bay. Even experienced speakers will often have a temporary feeling of regression when they stay away from speaking opportunities for some time.

Self-evaluation. An important part of your progress against stagefright will be your analysis of what happened during each of your speaking opportunities. After each presentation, think through or write down how you felt about what you did. Describe what you went through, what you did well and how you could have done a better job. Determine what you will do differently next time based upon your analysis. Your few moments of reflection will help you to be better prepared for stagefright the next time you feel it.

Congratulate yourself for all the things you did right and any positive feedback you received from others. Ask a member of the audience later for candid feedback on what they perceived. See what that person retained and what he or she does or thinks differently about because of your presentation. These activities are essential to making speaking to groups a natural, comfortable activity for you in the future.

Keep improving. Keep your plan for progress alive and seek to further improve your skills. Still try to do a good job, long after it is no longer difficult to do so. Be more critical of areas in which you can improve and pay greater attention to the details of your delivery. Challenge yourself with new audiences, circumstances and material and make speaking a life-long skill to develop.

I was recently giving a presentation that I had given many times before. I was using a humorous story that, as I spoke, I recalled did not go over very well the last time I had used it, although it had worked for many occasions before that. I had a sudden surge of panic that caused me to stumble a little. Probably because of my sudden doubt, the story did not go over well this time either! Had I taken time prior to the session to think through the example, I'm sure it would have been effective once again. The lesson: there is always room for improvement.

Enjoy yourself. Although this may seem difficult when you are scared of a speaking situation, sometimes you can push your way into enjoying the situation. Always smile, even if it is forced, or members of the audience are likely to think something is wrong. Humor is almost always appreciated by audiences and serves as a release for you and for them, as well as a means of picking up the energy level of the group. Tell yourself, "This isn't bad at all, in fact it's even a little fun." Soon you will actually believe it. When faced with a new speaking engagement, you will be off to the right start by responding: "It sounds like that would be fun."

Speaking without Fear

You may feel you have achieved your goal after you have conquered your fear, but be careful! Speaking wihtout fear brings with it its own problems. These attitudes and behaviors may be more detrimental than your worst symptoms from fear.

You may be boring. If you no longer have any fears about speaking, your anxiety level is apt to go down and you may slip into being totally unconcerned with how you come across to a group. You may ramble endlessly, not caring if you are understood.

You may be lazy. You should always respect your audience enough to do some preparation—even after you don't think you need it. Be humble about yourself and your speaking abilities. Always spend a certain amount of time checking and preparing your material for a presentation, even if the topic or the skill becomes second nature. Mentally walking through your presentation will help to make the actual presentation flow more smoothly and your audience will appreciate the fact that you are well prepared.

You may be obnoxious. You may start to insult the audience or act cocky and too self-assured. You might talk over their heads and not care if they understand or not.

To be successful at speaking to groups, I believe there should always remain a lingering tension about the occasion. If you are completely sure about yourself, the topic and the audience, you will lose sensitivity and flexibility in the situation. Those missing ingredients will show through in what is likely to appear as a "canned speech."

If you never have any nervousness about a speaking situation, chances are you are not using your speaking abilities to their fullest. If you only use your skill in "safe" circumstances, little growth will occur.

Helping Others with Speaking Fears

As you progress in your ability to overcome your speaking fears, you will be in a position to help others. You will know better than most people what the speaker is experiencing. You will also find that you learn fastest that which you teach, so your own fear will subside more easily as you focus on other people's fears of speaking.

Assume the fear. Take for granted that a person is nervous about speaking in front of a group. When a speaker is in front of you and you sit as a member of the audience, ask yourself if you would be nervous if you were in his or her position. If your answer is "yes," then assume that individual is probably nervous and might have a difficult time. Give him whatever support you can, such as by nodding approval.

As a member of an audience, you can feel removed from responsibility for the effectiveness of the presentation. You may expect to be entertained by the speaker and take a defensive "prove it to me" attitude. Change your perspective if you notice the speaker is having trouble. Instead of passively hoping that the speaker will not fail or criticizing the speaker's lack of preparation or degree of fear, take an active role to assist.

Alleviating stress. Do something to help take attention (and tension) off the speaker. In most groups, this can be done by asking an easy question or making a statement to support the points being discussed. In a larger group, you might lend support by reacting at appropriate times in appropriate ways as the speaker had hoped (laughing at jokes, for example) in order to give him or her encouragement.

To help others and yourself overcome stagefright, set up a network of individuals. These people can serve to talk through ideas for presentations, discuss the details of the presentation and serve as a mock audience for dry-run practice presentations. If you have access to video tape equipment, as many employers now do, you can work with someone in taping and evaluating your delivery.

Coaching can be done on a very informal basis with a friend or significant other, or it can become a routine part of your professional life by using peers, supervisors or subordinates to listen to and critique your performance.

A New Attitude and Potential

Conquering anxiety or fear you might have about presentational speaking *is* possible by taking an aggressive attitude about speaking. The first moment that you are asked to give a presentation, respond in a positive way with: "I'd be honored!" This will help to establish a positive, productive attitude toward that specific presentation and you will be less likely to avoid, dread, or procrastinate on your preparation for the task. A confident, aggressive approach to presentational speaking will keep most imagined fears from becoming a reality.

One day you will wake up and realize that you no longer are concerned or apprehensive about speaking situations. You will have arrived at the point of being a truly competent speaker. You will spend no more time worrying about or avoiding speaking situations. Your preparations will be very matter-of-fact and you will relish the new power and sensation that you receive in front of others, as well as the gratification that you are now able to assist many individuals more easily. This point will usually come sometime after you cannot remember how many presentations you have given. Speaking will have become a natural part of your day-to-day life and a valuable asset to your career.

Your new-found speaking skills will help to open new opportunities for you in both your personal and your professional lives. As you make more and more presentations, your speaking fears will fade to distant memories and you will smile slightly to yourself at how fearful you once were of an activity you now find exciting, fun, and rewarding.

Appendix
How to Prepare a Speech

Most of your fears about speaking will be significantly reduced if your presentation is properly prepared and practiced in advance. If you go into a speaking situation unprepared, you have every right to be scared. Without knowing what you are going to say, who you are saying it to, and what strategy you will use to effectively communicate your points, it is more likely you will falter. What follows is a straightforward guide to preparing a speech. It covers getting started, organizing your message, and practicing and revising your presentation. Also provided is a brief discussion on the use of visual aids and several worksheets which can be used for preparing speeches and for question-and-answer sessions, too.

Getting Started

Get started early. Giving a presentation will be a less awesome task if you get started on it early. As soon as you know you are going to give a presentation, jot down some ideas about the topic, some initial questions you have and information you need to collect. Block out time on your calendar for preparation and practice. Getting started early will keep you from being paralyzed by panic and give you momentum in your preparation efforts. You will not waste energy worrying and will avoid the mental block that often sets in when you feel time is running out.

Assess the situation. As soon as you know that you will be giving a presentation, clarify the variables of the situation, perhaps using the previously discussed Fear Map as a guide. What is expected? What is the occasion? How many will be in the audience? What time limits do you have? What comes prior to and after your presentation? What is your role in the overall situation? What points should be highlighted? Keep notes so you can refer to them in later stages of preparing your speech.

Typically you will be asked to speak on a topic in your specific area of expertise so that you can take advantage of your credibility and of what you already know. If the topic of the presentation is open to your discretion, ask yourself some more questions. Ask what would be most valuable or interesting for the audience to hear about, or ask yourself what topics you are most knowledgeable about. Often your best idea for a topic will be the first that comes to mind. It may be a subject you feel strongly about or something currently on your mind.

Make lists. First, list the significant points you want to cover in your presentation. If the audience will only remember two or three points the next day, what do you want those to be? What other information do you want to convey? This list will help you outline your speech, and will also indicate where you need to do further research.

Make another list of the items you need to prepare to be ready at the scheduled time. This list might include an outline, people to talk to, handouts to type up and run off, visual aids to prepare, and various stages of practice. Go back over this second list to see which items will take more time and need to be started sooner. If, for example, you want to use overhead transparencies, you will need to know the content of your presentation well in advance so you can decide what material to have converted into overheads. You will also need to arrange for a projector and screen (or clear wall space) for practice sessions as well as for the final presentation.

Organizing Your Message

There are certain components that must be built into every speech. If you skip any of them, you are apt to be less effective or to leave your audience confused. Make sure the following are included in every speech you give:

Attention-getter. When you begin your presentation, most individuals in the audience will not be waiting intently for your first words. More likely, they are planning the rest of the day's activities, determining who they need to telephone, or otherwise letting their attention wander. When their attention does focus on you, it will initially be to observe and evaluate you. Gradually they will "warm up" to your topic and what you have to say about it. If you begin presenting your information too quickly, before you have the complete attention of your audience, you will have probably lost a significant portion of your listeners. Because they missed your opening statement, they are not sure why you are there and where you are going in your speech. They will spend the remainder of your talk either trying to piece together what you are saying or simply going back to their previous train of thought—a much easier task for them to do. To have the group start together you must draw everyone's attention through one or more of the techniques discussed on pages 40–43.

Overview statement. Once you have captured the attention of the audience, tell them what you are going to say. The overview or thesis statement needs to be concise and precise. It makes an assertion which you hope to convince the audience is true by the end of your speech. It overviews the scope of your topical material and suggests the direction your presentation will follow. Here is an assortment of representative thesis statements.

> Absenteeism policies at our company need to be revised.
> Interest rates need to stabilize for industry to grow.

The family as a social unit is changing.
Federal regulations are stifling small businesses.
The crime rate is a factor that you can control.

Significance statement. Next, you need to explain why the topic is important to the group you are addressing. You need to help your audience make the mental transition from hearing the overview statement to understanding the impact it could have on their lives. Why should they listen? Why should they be concerned? What will happen if they are not concerned? You want to quickly and clearly draw the significance of the issue home to each person listening. For example, in the last sample overview statement listed above, a significance statement might be: "Each person in this room is likely to be a victim of some crime in the next five years."

Your overview and significance statements are so important to clear communication that you should have them both written down and/or committed to memory. There are only a few sentences in the typical presentation that require this word-for-word exacting delivery.

Key points. The body of your speech should be made up of the information that is essential for your audience to retain. These key points can serve as the outline of your speech. Plan on communicating two or three points per five to seven minutes of presentation time. Each of the key points should be supported by two or three pieces of evidence. The evidence can take the form of statistics, newspaper reports, stories, or results from studies, surveys, interviews, or previous meetings. If you can see that you need to obtain additional supporting evidence, make a note of that on your list of things to do.

Transitions. Transitional statements are as important as the points you make. Transitions provide the logical flow from one statement to the next and serve as connecting bridges between key points. If you do not have them, you will leave a portion of your audience behind trying to figure out how a seemingly new topic relates to what you had just been saying. For example: "The first reason why crime concerns you has to do with protecting your property, but of even greater importance is the second reason..." Transitions and the points they connect should be stated more slowly and louder than the other information in your speech. Write out your transitions word for word so there will be little chance that you will forget them.

Summary and conclusion. A good summary reviews the major points that were made and, if appropriate, leaves the audience with a clear sense of what is expected of them. One technique is to tie the close of the speech back to the opening attention-getting statement. Never end by saying "That's all." Have the specific wording of your close planned in advance so that you know when and how you will stop.

Objections and questions. After you have made a rough draft of your presentation, you need to examine your draft from the audience's perspective and consider what objections and questions audience members are likely to raise. If an objection is significant, it should be addressed in the body of your speech. You should be able to anticipate and have an answer prepared for all the questions you are likely to be asked. Prepare for questions you can't answer with a response such as: "That's an excellent question. I don't know the answer, but I'll find out and get back to you."

You have passed the difficult portion of your preparation once you have thought the key points through and roughly organized your speech. Now, simply fill in the skeleton of your outline with the necessary supporting information and details. Most information can be written in abbreviated notes to yourself. The main points—overview and significance statements, key points, transitions, and closing—should be written out word for word.

Your delivery should be made from a skeletal outline of your presentation. This outline can all be on one page or it can be divided between several note cards. Try several methods to see which one is the most comfortable for you and the least disruptive to the communication process. Avoid flimsy paper because it is apt to rustle as you hold or move it. Number index cards if you use them in case you drop them or get them out of sequence.

Practice and Revisions

People especially dread presenting information to a group the first time. If they have occasion to repeat the same information to another group at another time, it is a much easier task. After several such presentations of the same topic, especially if the presentations are close to one another, there is usually no anxiety at all. The trick, then, is to make the first "live" presentation actually the third or fourth, from your perspective. Begin by practicing in low-risk situations to work the trouble spots out of your presentation. Then gradually work up to simulating as closely as possible the speaking situation you will be encountering.

You will need to schedule specific times to practice. In fact, you should spend about five times as much time practicing as you have spent in preparing to this point so you can work out any problems and gain cofidence for the real presentation. Practice the sub-routines that make up your entire speech—the start and close, the points you want to stress, and the parts you are uncomfortable with until they all join together into a performance you can be proud of.

The first practice drafts should simply focus on getting through the material comfortably in a steady flow. Here are five progressive steps you can take to make your practice sessions as easy and effective as possible.

1. Your mental draft. Perhaps the simplest and most non-threatening way to review your presentation is to think it through. Get in a comfortable position, perhaps in an easy chair or lying down in bed. Close your eyes and think through your presentation. Imagine hearing yourself being introduced, walking up to the podium, and looking out at faces in the audience. Imagine the actual words you would use as you deliver your speech. Refer to your notes as often as needed.

If this is a difficult task for you, you can skip it and attempt another type of practice, or you may want to go into greater detail with this step. For some people, a smooth flow of infor-

mation comes more readily when they write down what they want to say. This does not mean the presentation should be memorized; instead, it should only provide one way of wording the information for the first practice. Hopefully, each practice will both improve the way information could be presented and increase the number of ways that the ideas could be described.

2. **Your speaking draft.** After you have mentally gone through your presentation, attempt going over the presentation verbally. Still strive for a nonthreatening practice: remain seated and just talk out loud as you go down your outline. At this stage you can even practice as you are showering, jogging or driving a car. Remember to keep what you are saying in the first person, for example, say: "It's an important problem we have to discuss today, one that affects each and every one of us," rather than talking to yourself and saying, "Then I'll tell them about how important the problem is. . ." Your goal is to use the actual words, or a variety thereof, that will be used in your real presentation.

3. **Your standing draft.** After a couple of times through your talking draft, attempt the same practice technique, but stand up. Make a mock podium, if you will eventually have one, for your final presentation, and begin to fill in the behavior portion of your message, that is: your gestures, eye contact, and other types of nonverbal behavior. Just as you do not memorize words, do not memorize gestures. Specifically practiced gestures almost always come across as staged and thus artificial. Instead, try a variety of gestures that are natural to you. It is more important for you to become comfortable with your physical space around you and your ability to gesture in general, than to try to mimic any specific gesture. Do this by overgesturing; that is, amplifying your gestures and trying new ones. Wave your arms, point, stretch, pound your fist, grip your hands. Experiment to see what you find is effective for

your style. At first they might all seem contrived, but with practice and less inhibition, natural gesturing will spring forth from your style.

4. **Audience draft**. If you hate speaking to groups, I can guarantee you that you will hate to *practice* speaking to groups. But you need to do so. You can only improve a skill by doing that skill. Practice your draft in front of a friend or audience member. Practice it with that person until you are comfortable, then practice before a new individual or a small group. Seek suggestions for improvement after each session, and revise your presentation as needed.

5. **Final rehearsal**. Prior to giving the actual presentation, do a dress rehearsal, duplicating the real situation as closely as possible. Wear the same clothes you plan to wear, practice at the same time of day, use the visual aids you will be using, and —if possible—have a member or two of the real audience sit in on this practice session.

Using Visual Aids

You may find it helpful to use some type of visual aid in your presentation. The simplest, a small card with your key points listed on it, will help keep you on track as you deliver your speech. More elaborate visual aids are shared with the audience, and have the further value of keeping the audience's attention, reinforcing your verbal message, and making it possible to explain difficult concepts or procedures. Visual aids should never replace the speech itself, however, and need to be carefully selected and prepared in advance. If you are going to use visual aids, be sure to include them in your practice sessions. Here are some of the most commonly used visual aids:

Note cards. Your notes are, of course, helpful for remembering your organization and key points. Be careful not to have too many notes, because you are apt to lose your place. You should be able to get all the notes you will need for a five- to seven-minute talk on a single 5 × 7-inch note card. Avoid having paper that rustles when you move it.

Overhead slides. Some speakers simply place their notes on overhead slides and systematically go through them with the audience. You are less apt to lose your place and can devote more energy looking directly at your audience, instead of down at notes. It is also possible to uncover a single point at a time on the overhead, thus controlling the pace of the presentation and the attention of the group.

Flip charts. Notes can also be pre-written on a flip chart. In this case, lighter, penciled comments may be written that only you can read while standing next to the easel.

Handouts. If you are nervous, a handout would be of great assistance. One advantage of a handout is that it can be redone numerous times until it says exactly what you want to relate to the group. Your major points can be clearly stated on the paper to help your audience follow your presentation as well. Don't pass out the handout until you want audience members to look at it because they will immediately read it when it is distributed.

35mm slides. For the professional presentation, slides will help assure your message is communicated well. They are entertaining and can provide an extensive amount of information visually in a short amount of time. Attention of the audience, however, will diminish when the lights are turned down. Slides are more expensive, as well.

Preliminary Arrangements Checklist

Date & Time:_____

Room _____ # Expected _____

Seating Arrangement:

Auditorium_____   Classroom_____   Informal_____

U-Shape_____ Other_____

	OK	Needs Attention	Comments:
Chairs			
Tables			
Lighting			
Ventilation			
Distractions			
Ash trays			
Pencils/Scratch paper			
Name cards			
Coffee/soft drinks/water			
Handouts			
Electrical accessories (bulb/cord/plug/extension)			
Audio-visual equipment			
Supplies (chalk/eraser felt pens/grease pencil/tape)			
Audience notification			

Presentation Worksheet

Attention-getting statement:_____

_____

_____

Overview statement: _____

_____

_____

Significance statement: _____

_____

_____

Key points:

1) _____

_____

2) _____

_____

3) _____

_____

Speech body.

Key point #1: _____

_____

_____

Supporting evidence:_____

_____

_____

Transition: _____

_____

_____

Key point #2: _____

_____

_____

Supporting evidence: _____

_____

_____

Transition: _____

_____

_____

Key point #3: _____

_____

_____

Supporting evidence: _____

_____

_____

Transition: _____

_____

_____

Summary: _____

_____

_____

Review of key points:

1)_____
_____
_____

2)_____
_____
_____

3)_____
_____
_____

Conclusion:_____
_____
_____

Probable objections audience members will have:

Objection #1: _____
_____

Objection #2: _____
_____

Objection #3: _____
_____

Probable questions you will receive:

Question #1: _____

_____

    Your answer: _____

    _____

Question #2: _____

_____

    Your answer: _____

    _____

Question #3: _____

_____

    Your answer: _____

    _____

Question #4: _____

_____

    Your answer: _____

    _____

Question #5: _____

_____

    Your answer: _____

    _____

Question #6: _____

_____

    Your answer: _____

    _____

Question #7: _____

_____

   Your answer: _____

_____

Question #8: _____

_____

   Your answer: _____

_____

Question #9: _____

_____

   Your answer: _____

_____

Question #10: _____

_____

   Your answer: _____

_____

Additional Fear Map

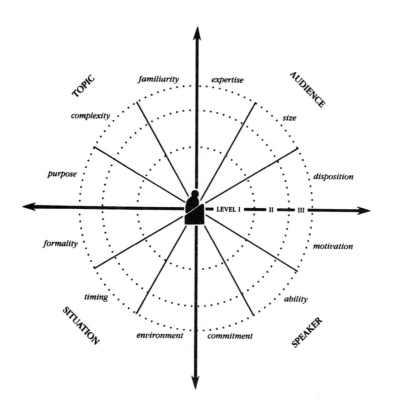

Presentation Worksheet

Attention-getting statement:_____

_____

_____

Overview statement: _____

_____

_____

Significance statement: _____

_____

_____

Key points:

1) _____

_____

2) _____

_____

3) _____

_____

Speech body.

Key point #1: _____

_____

_____

Supporting evidence:_____

_____

_____

Transition: _____

_____

_____

Key point #2: _____

_____

_____

Supporting evidence: _____

_____

_____

Transition: _____

_____

_____

Key point #3: _____

_____

_____

Supporting evidence: _____

_____

_____

Transition: _____

_____

_____

Summary: _____

_____

_____

Review of key points:

1)_____

_____

_____

2)_____

_____

_____

3)_____

_____

_____

Conclusion:_____

_____

_____

Probable objections audience members will have:

Objection #1: _____

_____

Objection #2: _____

_____

Objection #3: _____

_____

Probable questions you will receive:

Question #1: _____

_____

   Your answer: _____

_____

Question #2: _____

_____

   Your answer: _____

_____

Question #3: _____

_____

   Your answer: _____

_____

Question #4: _____

_____

   Your answer: _____

_____

Question #5: _____

_____

   Your answer: _____

_____

Question #6: _____

_____

   Your answer: _____

_____

Question #7: _____

_____

   Your answer: _____

_____

Question #8: _____

_____

   Your answer: _____

_____

Question #9: _____

_____

   Your answer: _____

_____

Question #10: _____

_____

   Your answer: _____

_____

Additional Fear Map

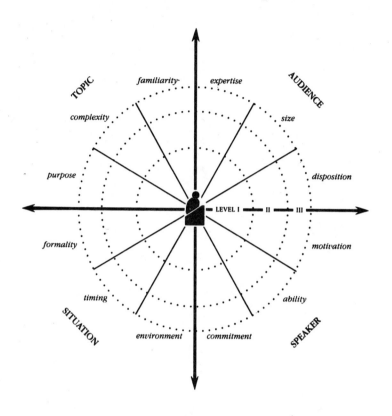

About the Author

Robert B. Nelson has done extensive public speaking before audiences of 20 to 4000 as well as on radio and television. He has taught stagefright and public speaking courses and helped numerous individuals overcome their fear of speaking before others. He is a past member of the St. Paul Metropolitan Toastmasters and a charter member of the Minneapolis Downtown YMCA Toastmasters. This is his third book of public speaking.

May we introduce other Ten Speed Press books you may find useful . . .
over three million people have already.

What Color Is Your Parachute? by Richard N. Bolles
The Truth Option by Will Schutz
The Damn Good Resume Guide by Yana Parker
The Three Boxes of Life by Richard N. Bolles
Where Do I Go From Here With My Life?
by John C. Crystal and Richard N. Bolles
Who's Hiring Who by Richard Lathrop
Don't Use a Resume by Richard Lathrop
Mail Order Know-How by Cecil C. Hoge, Sr.
Mail Order Moonlighting by Cecil C. Hoge, Sr.
The Student Entrepreneur's Guide by Brett M. Kingstone
Computer Wimp by John Bear
Better Letters by Jan Venolia
Write Right! by Jan Venolia
Finding Facts Fast by Alden Todd

You will find them in your bookstore or library,
or you can send for our *free* catalog:

TEN SPEED PRESS
P O Box 7123   Berkeley, California 94707